At last a values-based approach for pa
family values, self-regulation and respect for self and others as strategies to raise
a capable and confident person; traits that will protect them and serve them
well online and off.

This book is a must-read for any parent wanting to develop resiliency in
their child and to empower them in today's hyper-connected world.

Sir Gordon Tietjens KNZM

I believe in fate. A few weeks ago I was asked by John to read his book *Keeping
Your Children Safe Online*. The reason I say 'fate' is because I had noticed my
teenager withdrawing from our family. Even when we watched TV together I
noticed she was tucked away on her phone and laptop.

I hadn't known how to approach this topic as I didn't do a good job the first
time when she was younger, being that technology, especially the platforms
she used, are foreign to me, such as the social platforms being used to connect
millions of people; information is instant and graphic.

Your name and what you do is there for anyone to see. Fate has allowed
my wife, our children and me to have a much better understanding around
the world of the 'cybernauts' and our role as parents, to support, encourage
and guide them on their life journeys. Core family values, open and respectful
conversations, collaborative understanding around online boundaries.

The key message I got from reading this book was that we as parents are
crucial to keeping our children safe online. Be conscious of what we do and
then say, be present, and when a mistake happens, let them know you love
them, they are unique and there is only one of them in the world; remember
you are not alone. Thank you, John, for the insight, the wisdom, the stories and
tools. I highly recommend this book to every parent and young person so you
can traverse the online world together.

Norm Hewitt, Team Culture and Leadership Development
'Hoe tahi Tatau, let us row together'

The cyber world is here, like it or not, it's not going anywhere. We have two
choices in this life as parents, educators, as citizens – we can resist change
and growth, tell ourselves that it won't last or it's not healthy and refuse to
participate. Or, we can learn to embrace it, to use it for the purpose it was
intended; to open our horizons and allow us all to extend ourselves and
participate globally ... John teaches us how to go with option two.

I would recommend this book to anyone who has young people in their lives
who are learning and growing in our technological world. John Parsons connects
with people in this book as he does in his workshops and presentations.

It's easy to read, sensible and practical and it brings us technology as a tool for communication, as well as a reminder of how precious our children and young people are.

Cheryl Smeaton, Adult Community Educator

As an Emergency physician I have witnessed the terrible consequences of cyber-bullying. As a parent I am exasperated by the magnetic pull the internet has on my kids. John Parsons offers parents a highly crafted skill set we could never have conceived the need for even two decades ago. This is an important piece of work written by an exceptional man whose intelligent humour and extraordinary levels of energy infect all those who meet him. I am the better for knowing him.

Dr Andrew Munro, Emergency Medicine Specialist

Four years ago John presented an internet-safety course to young people aged 10 to 12. Part of his message was around Criteria: how they could judge normal/safe adult behaviours that made sense to a young person. In particular, 'Would your doctor or dentist behave like this? Would they want to be your friend on Facebook?' This critical message was applied over a year later by a vulnerable child in a difficult situation; the child remembered John's message and made a choice that kept him safe. The adult concerned was subsequently convicted for crimes against children, but thankfully this student was *not* a victim because of the course he had taken with John Parsons.

Since then I have invited John to work with a number of schools, and I've observed students, parents and teachers becoming better informed and more confident in how to manage digital technology at home and within the school. I am so pleased he has written a book as this enables many more people to access this very important information.

Bev Moore, Statutory Services provider for Ministry of Education

I have been privileged to know John since he started delivering his cyber-safety programme in our Southland community. A wonderful, caring man, helping to keep our community safe. A fabulous example of someone making a difference where it matters. In the words of one participant, 'This man is pure gold!'

Karen Purdue, Invercargill Sunrise Rotary Club

For many the cyber-world of our children can be a place foreign to us as adults. Teenagers often disconnect with parents when they are at their most vulnerable, but John's message is clear: 'Travel with and protect your child'. This is an amazing book and an essential read.

Douglas McLean, Principal, Whakatane Intermediate School

I have the utmost esteem for John and this work. I have observed the development of his enterprise since its inception and believe his contribution to this nation is unequalled in its integrity and morality. John's passion and skill for this work is obvious, his highly ethical care and aroha for the people with whom he works is unquestionable. This practical, reassuring and useful resource will be warmly received by parents, teachers and health professionals with eager anticipation to activate his wisdom, skill and experience.

Kindra Douglas, Director, Victory Community Centre, Nelson

John is an inspiring man who is passionate about making the world a better and safer place for our children. His dedication to cyber-safety education in the secondary school sector is to be commended. It has been an honour and privilege to work with John.

Jennifer Dalton, Year 9 Dean, Nelson College for Girls

John, this is truly a book for our time. You have offered support for parents and caregivers in a no-nonsense, straightforward way. It is very evident you see this not as an IT issue but as a health and safety one. Not only is it a good read, but it will continue to be a handy reference book as the internet and social media develop.

Senior Constable John O'Donovan QSM, New Zealand Police (Retired)

John Parsons's impassioned drive to shine decency and respect into the potentially dark and risky world of cyber-space has saved children's lives. I can state this with impunity as I have witnessed so in my field as a trauma therapist. I have seen families come together, rather than implode, in the face of discovering that their child has inadvertently fallen into a snare set by an on-line predator. And I have heard from children, and my own family members, of how inspired they are by John's approach to keeping them safe from harm. John has the perfect balance of compassion, respect and know-how to make a massive impact on child safety, not only in New Zealand, but worldwide. This book encapsulates John's unique and proven approach beautifully.

Briar Haven, Manager, Nelson Sexual Abuse Counselling Services (NSACS) Ltd.

This is the book I've been waiting for – sound, practical advice as we guide the children in our lives to safety through the complexities of an online world. I've seen John advise parents whose teenage son would probably not be alive without his knowledge. As one boy said, 'I did what you said and I kept myself safe.' We all have a part to play – read this book!

Annette Milligan, Director, INP Medical Clinic

Jam-packed with ideas, John cuts to the chase like no-one else. I know his work makes a real difference for people who attend his talks and who consult him about difficult situations. I am glad he now has it in a book which is so heartwarmingly readable. I will be recommending it to clients, colleagues, friends and family.

Geoffrey Samuels, Clinical Psychologist

This book is rigorous, ethical and transformative. Written in very accessible language, it is practical, informative and thorough. Every parent/caregiver will feel resourced and supported as they read this book, and I encourage them to actively engage with their children in what it offers. I unequivocally support John's wisdom and deep experience in this challenging work.

Liz Price, Counsellor and Family Therapist, Supervisor and Trainer

I first heard John speak at a Teachers Only Day. His presentation was outstanding, with incredibly informative content regarding cyber-safety and the issues of social media for our children. From this, I booked John to speak with our students and we have had him return to our school on an annual basis, such is the importance and credibility we place on his knowledge and information. John relates exceptionally well to the children and presents the content in a meaningful and humorous manner. All schools should invest in John presenting to their students, to better inform and make our children aware of safe internet and social media use.

Regan Orr, Principal, Fairfield School, Levin

John's wonderful humour and warmth are very evident in this practical guide to staying safe online. John's annual visits to talk to our students are essential in empowering them to make good decisions and to build strong relationships. It's a message of hope – our values really can keep us safe.

Richard Barnett, Associate Principal, Burnside High School, Christchurch

Over the past eight years our school has been working with John, both in student and parent workshops. He has brought a wealth of experience and knowledge to guide and support parents. Every parent, student and teacher leaves these workshops with immediate skills they can implement both in their personal and work lives. The strategies given by John, and now set out in this book in practical and accessible language, will give everyone the confidence to support the children and teenagers in their lives, to manage themselves in an online world.

Lucy Feltham, Head Teacher, Nelson College for Girls Preparatory School

I have worked with John for the last five years in the education system where his knowledge, skills and genuine passion for the well-being of our young people of New Zealand has demanded action from schools to look more closely at the areas of cyber safety and protection.

John's presentations are engaging with a message that connects not only with our students but also our teachers and parents to ensure that as we live in an ever-changing technological world, it is one that we understand and doesn't mitigate the values we have.

This book is one that all schools should have as it provides the backgrounds, ideas and structures that will support all educators in managing the cyber-world.

Simon Coleman, Principal, Geraldine High School, South Canterbury

Every NZ school kid – and their parents – needs to hear the John Parsons message: ideally, more than once. The cyber world is a minefield for the unwary: John Parsons' work is the best and most accessible personal cyber-protection going: that's why he is in our school on an annual basis. This book captures those messages for parents and they need to read it.

Kerry Hawkins, Principal, Waverley Park School, Invercargill

John has worked in the school for a number of years to support our school health education programme and in particular helping students keep themselves cyber-safe. His presentations, which cover a range of internet issues are always well constructed, relevant and delivered in such a way as to have an impact on our students as they move forward into adolescence.

As a school we see John's involvement as an integral component of our overall health education. For those of you who have not had the opportunity to hear John speak, I heartily recommend his new book as a guide for parenting in a world dominated by the internet.

Henk Popping, Principal, Otumoetai Intermediate School, Tauranga

If you want practical guidance and take-away strategies to keep your children safe online then step right this way and read *Keeping Your Children Safe Online*.

As someone who has worked on the front line for over 30 years and as a parent myself I can't recall meeting anyone who is more qualified and experienced to write a book on cyber safety than John. This will be the most vital parenting book you will ever need.

Willow Duffy, General Manager, Safeguarding Children

Dedication

To my wife, thank you for supporting me, challenging me and encouraging me to keep this book on track – I could not do any of this without you. You are the best thing that has ever happened to me.

To my three wonderful daughters: as a teenager, I was mostly angry and lost. If somebody back then could have told me how happy I would be right now because I have people like you in my life, I would not have believed them. You are my life, and I am so very proud of you.

To Mum and Dad, you gave me the best start in life. The love, compassion and kindness you gave me I now pass on to your grandchildren. You have influenced me in this book. I lost you at age 13 and found you in the eyes and smiles of my children.

KEEPING YOUR CHILDREN SAFE
ONLINE

A Guide for New Zealand Parents

JOHN PARSONS

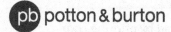

pb potton & burton

The following terms used in this book are trademarked
and hold trademark certificates:

Cyber Separation
Cybernaut
Cyber Muscles
Cyber Tooth Tiger
Digital Boundary
Digital Boundary, Family, Friends, Self
Safe Circle, Family, Friends, Me

First published in 2017 by Potton & Burton
98 Vickerman Street, PO Box 5128, Nelson, New Zealand
pottonandburton.co.nz

Text © John Parsons

Edited by Jude Watson

ISBN 978 0 947503 44 4

Printed in New Zealand by printing.com

CONTENTS

Mā te huruhuru ka rere te manu
Adorn the bird with feathers so it may fly

PREFACE

My father said to me, 'No matter what you do in life, you will always be my son and I will always love you.' My mother said to me, 'If you are about to eat food and the person in front of you has no food, divide the meal and give them half, then nobody goes hungry.'

My mother and father died when I was 13 years old, but these two statements never left me. I knew they loved me, I knew they cared ... in a child's world, everything else comes in second.

This book has been written for all parents and caregivers who want to keep their child safe when they are online. It outlines the skills and strategies necessary to empower your child so that they can protect themselves and have boundaries when using the myriad digital devices and platforms available to them.

It's important to know that this book does not require you to be skilled in the use of information technology or to have any particular expertise in the online world. All that is required is for you to believe that the answer to keeping your children safe in the digital world starts with them having a strong sense of self-worth, of knowing they are valuable individuals.

Cyber-safety education has, in my opinion, focused too much on developing technical knowledge and not enough on how we can project the family values we use every day in the physical world in to the online world as well.

I have been working frontline in online child protection and cyber-safety for over ten years. Much of this work has been helping to support individual victims of cyber-crime, and this has resulted in the development of educational material and workshops now used widely by teachers, students, parents and health professionals throughout New Zealand.

Always at the end of parent workshops and professional development sessions I am asked if there is any material they can take away that captures my approach to these issues. This book is my response. It is based wholly on experience. The stories, with names changed, are real, and in many instances have involved agencies that have contributed to successful outcomes for the child. All of my work in the area of cyber-safety is collaborative, and I want to acknowledge the parents, teachers, police officers, health professionals, and above all the brave young people and their families, who have helped increase my knowledge and encouraged me in this work.

My most important message to any parent or guardian reading this book is that if you are raising your child in an environment where family values based on respect and empathy are present, then you already have the foundation to support your child online. Take heart.

By tapping into the strength of your existing family bonds, you can readily build your child's understanding and skills to ensure they will learn to act responsibly and protect themselves, their family and their friends in the online world. And as with any parenting situations we face, remember to just apply wisdom and logic to the decisions you make. There may be strategies set out here that are not achievable in the way I suggest, so just shape them to your needs or find alternatives that work for your family. Values are constants; how we realise them is not.

John Parsons
May 2017

INTRODUCTION

People are driven to share ideas, to gossip, laugh together, to debate, to argue, to learn – communication is the lifeblood of any functioning society.

Is it any wonder that people flock to the internet? It is the largest gathering space that has ever been created, and we love it. It allows for the most extraordinary diversity of communication, and it feeds our drive to explore, to express ourselves and to learn about our world and our universe.

Young people especially need to learn to communicate in order to grow, be challenged, feel valued, form friendships and learn about themselves. Social media, online gaming platforms and applications where they can be challenged and play give young people opportunities to interact with the world.

Today, the final barrier that binds most of us to one place – distance – has been eliminated by computers and the internet. Our children are constantly moving through cyberspace from one location to another with very little overhead and at no cost. They communicate with people they will never meet in person, from many different cultures, and they will share ideas with them, debate and argue, all from their mobile screens. Your children are this generation's explorers, 'cybernauts', who flock to the internet and travel through cyberspace in their millions every day.

Digital communication technology (DCT) is an extraordinary tool, and the powerful light it shines on the world allows us to experience far more than we once could, both good and bad. **Our challenge as parents is to ensure that positive aspects of the online world are maximised and negative aspects minimised,** based on our children's age and level of maturity.

The negative side of the internet is very real, with the news full of examples of cyber-crime aimed at senior citizens, sexual predators targeting children, cyber-bullying, and online scams in the private sector becoming more and more sophisticated. It's no wonder some parents dread the day when their 11-year-old asks, 'Can I have a smart phone? All my friends have one.' Whatever you may wish, telling them they have to wait until they leave home is not an option.

As our children approach adolescence, the choice we have is whether or not to follow them into cyberspace. If we do, I believe it offers us the best opportunity to assist and support them in keeping themselves and others safe.

Regardless of our views, they *will* use digital technology, as the desire to communicate is very powerful. In the face of this, **our goal should be to empower our children to live in the online world safely and ethically**. Cyber-safety education delivered by parents within the home, in an environment of parental support and trust, is the most effective option we have. And a crucial part of building trust is the parental acknowledgement of a young person's right to communicate online. This is essential if you want to be alongside your child to help them learn to navigate this technology safely.

The two most important rooms in a healthy democracy are the living room and the classroom, and both require teachers. The single biggest influencer on how your child uses technology is you, and the best possible way for you to approach this relationship is from a place of trust and respect.

Digital technology both connects us with the rest of the world and disconnects us at the same time. Now, more than ever, we need to nurture empathy in our children. The ability to think about how another person is feeling is a vital tool children require as they navigate the digital space. **We need to be teaching our young people that they have a responsibility not only for the well-being of the person sitting next to them in the classroom but also for the person on the end of the device with whom they are communicating**.

This book is divided into two parts. Part One will turn you into a home-based cyber-safety teacher by taking your existing parental skills and updating them for a digital age. It introduces you to the fundamental concepts and strategies that a child needs to stay safe online, including how to transfer family values into the online environment, how to create digital boundaries around family and friends and self, and how to be in charge and project confidence in the digital space. These concepts and strategies are simple and practical, and once you have understood them you will be well on your way to a safer online world for you and your family.

Part Two focuses on the more specific risks young people can face, including sexual predation, sexting, cyber-bullying, cyber-crime, long-term damage to their reputation, and addiction to online gaming and pornography. Each of these issues presents particular challenges, and this book provides strategies to deal with them. It also provides advice for what to do when a risk becomes actual harm and you have a child who is a victim of a poor choice, circumstance or crime.

It is my hope that your child will learn through you that there is only one of them on the planet, that they are invaluable and, as with every generation, it's OK to make a mistake.

We need to step back from the digital platforms our child may use, whether it be Instagram, Facebook, Snapchat or an online game, and ask ourselves what fundamental values does he or she need to reduce risk or harm to themselves or others in this digital environment? I believe that you will find the answers in this book.

Some definitions within this book:

1. Mobile phones and the internet offer two distinct ways we can use digital technology to communicate with others. The motivation for people to use technology in most instances is to communicate with somebody known or unknown and/or receive communication. We are either broadcasting or receiving information when using mobile phones and the internet, and whilst they are different, they both share the same purpose: to communicate. In this book, I refer as little as possible to mobile phones or the internet, preferring to use 'online'. In most situations, the device or space being used by your child is irrelevant, because in this book we are focusing on *what* we communicate and *who* we communicate with, rather than the device or space used to do so.

2. You as the parent: I have chosen to generally use the term 'parent' in this book, but for each and every one of you who play this vital role in a child's life, know that you are acknowledged and respected for the task you've undertaken. I define 'parent' as 'any adult in close proximity to a child, being responsible for them or having the ability to protect them should they be in harm's way'.

PART 1

CHAPTER 1

FAMILY VALUES

Anchoring your child to what's important

Resilient children are those who learn how to deal with the challenges and problems that life throws at them, and in the context of this book, they are the ones who will develop the skills and strategies to keep themselves, and their family and friends, safe online as well as offline.

We cannot keep our children away from digital technology and we cannot watch over every corner of their lives. We can however teach them about appropriate boundaries, about how to project power and confidence, and ultimately how to integrate good values and decency into all parts of their lives offline and online.

There are three steps in keeping young people safe online:

- educating them to understand the value of self

- educating them to respect and protect family and friends

- educating them to broadcast decency and positive values across the internet

Protecting young people from the dangers they are exposed to in cyberspace is not found through developing a high level of technical understanding about the digital world. It is found by the child when they realise how invaluable they are as a person – in other words, when they find **a strong sense of self-worth**. They will also need self-control, compassion, empathy – all of the values that can be found in a home that nurtures, loves and protects their child. In coping with the online world, **the most important relationship a child has is the one with their family, not with the technology.**

Family values are things we live by but rarely discuss. You can see them expressed every day by the people you share your lives with. Many of these values have been passed down through the generations, and in turn we pass them on to our children. Children who grow up in homes that value love, empathy, compassion, tolerance, self-control and who support collectivism (living a life that includes supporting others and the community in which they live) will generally go on to live successful, meaningful lives.

I see the results of this in children and young people in schools across New Zealand every day: children playing happily and laughing with others, teenagers laughing at themselves, supporting others in times of need, welcoming new students into their circle of friends, and accepting other people's opinions and beliefs. And with all of these well-balanced children and teenagers, the most significant trait that they share is their ability to self-regulate their behaviour.

I will never forget the day a 16-year-old boy came up to me after a workshop, shook my hand and said, 'They never leave you, do they.' When I asked who, he replied, 'The people we love'. He went on to explain that he'd had an argument with another student at lunchtime that day, which almost erupted into a fight. He said, 'It was stupid, it was over a girl we both liked.' She was his ex-girlfriend and the student he'd argued with was her new boyfriend.

'How did you avoid the fight?' I asked.

'I walked off because I had my mum in my ear.' He said his mum didn't like seeing people fight or becoming angry and it scared her. 'Those conversations of hers often pop into my mind when I'm under stress,' he said. During the argument he could feel his anger building; he didn't like himself in that moment and he just walked off. As the argument progressed, he found he was becoming inconsistent with his mother's values. More importantly, they were now *his* values. His mother had tragically passed away two years earlier. The people we love never really leave us.

The digital world has a complicated, often mysterious, architecture and as a result, parents commonly believe when teaching a child to be safe online, they need a set of parenting skills different to the ones they use in the offline world. This has been further reinforced by cyber-safety education that focuses on functional and technical competency.

I've watched well-meaning cyber-safety presenters deliver workshops to parents and caregivers on how to use Instagram safely, how to turn on the privacy settings on Facebook and how to take screen shots on the latest iPhone – all of which can be found on Google within minutes at

My 11-year-old boy started acting strange, he wouldn't talk to us, he started spending more time in his bedroom and he stopped taking food to school. This went on for about a month. One evening I got a call from my brother. He was concerned about something he had seen on my son's Facebook page. They're friends in cyberspace. My boy had posted a picture of himself with the words 'I'm sick of living, my life sucks and school is horrible'.

I sat down with my boy and told him what his uncle had mentioned to me. He burst into tears and told me that four boys at school were bullying him and taking his food, one boy had ripped his jacket and punched him. The next day the school and the local police were informed of this and it was dealt with.

Children need family offline and online. If my brother wasn't connected to my boy we may not have found out about this as quickly as we did. We can be part of our child's online world. We just need to follow them out there – better still, be waiting for them when they arrive.

My brother lives in Africa and we live in Timaru.

Mother and new Facebook user

home. But parents/caregivers can leave such workshops disempowered and still feel they can't teach their child to be safe online because they themselves don't understand Instagram or they think Facebook is a waste of time or they don't know how Snapchat actually works.

Parents need to overcome the barriers they have built around themselves and simply get involved with their child online. Don't try to be an IT expert, that's not needed. Just jump onboard, get online, and then you'll see what they really need is you standing alongside them.

Respect is one of the main themes in my cyber-safety workshops. **People who demonstrate respect contribute to building a society that values other people's opinions even when they don't agree with them**. It is easier to trust a person we respect, and a person who is respectful is influential in their own social circles and the wider community. A child who learns respect has the ability to listen, to learn, to communicate. Respect is powerful. We power up our children when we teach them to respect others and the world in which they live. Respect is contagious and it needs to be modelled.

When Sarah was nine, she recalls her parents taking lots of photos of her, mostly at Christmas and on birthdays. She loved having her picture taken, even though there were a few she wished weren't online, as she didn't like the way she looked. She also remembers when they brought home her baby brother from the hospital, her mum took a photo of her naked three-day-old baby and posted it online for family and friends to see.

Sarah, now 12, is at school and she takes a picture of her friend Lily, and sends it to her other friends on Snapchat. The picture shows Lily looking embarrassed because her skirt has ripped up one side and she is doing her best to hold it together, while others are standing around laughing. Lily didn't know the picture had been taken. Later that evening Lily's mum calls Sarah's mum and explains that Lily is upset and feels let down by Sarah, as she took the picture of her friend without asking, posted it online, and as a result people are now laughing at her.

Sarah's mother sees the mistake her child has made but does not connect her behaviour back to how they as parents have modelled photo-taking. If parents want children to be safe online, then they need to model the same ethical behaviour they expect of their children when their children use digital technology.

For example, if from around age five or six, when Sarah's parents had taken pictures of her they had turned the camera around and asked her which images she liked and which ones she'd like deleted, this may have influenced how Sarah uses her mobile phone at school with her friends.

At around eight or nine years old, if Sarah's parents had started asking permission before taking a picture of her, how would that change Sarah's ethics when taking her own photos in the future? If Sarah grows up in a society where permission is not required before taking pictures, how can we judge Sarah when she doesn't seek permission? **The sooner we give children the right to say yes or no, the sooner we empower them**. This will contribute to a child valuing themselves and others, both online or offline.

Teaching a child to seek permission before taking a picture is an example of how an essential family value, respect, can be applied to their behaviour online. When the idea of respect is no longer just a concept in our child's mind but a tangible way of behaving, we can see that they, and society, will benefit.

And perhaps, when Sarah is 12 and being bombarded with inappropriate text messages from friends daring her, just for a laugh, to take a naked picture of herself, the fact that every time her parents had taken pictures of her they'd asked permission might help her to make the right decision. In those moments they would have been teaching Sarah that **her identity has value, that she owns it, that she has power, control and influence over what is done with it**.

When Sarah turns 13, she is now allowed to use Facebook, the minimum age required to join. She had in fact asked her dad if she could join when she was 12, but he had pointed out that to do this would require her to lie. He told her that her date of birth is so precious, they celebrate it once a year. 'If we allow you to lie about your real date of birth, that wouldn't help you understand how valuable your identity is.'

Her dad asked Sarah to imagine if Facebook was a physical place on the edge of town. There is no way he would give her permission to go and lie to the manager's face about her age. Why is it different when online? As well, there is the issue of simply respecting a business's own rules and regulations. Just because Facebook is online doesn't mean we should disrespect it.

This example highlights how family values from the offline world can be transferred to the online world. When Sarah does create a Facebook account, turns on the privacy settings and only accepts friends into her networks, she is reflecting her own sense of self-worth and her family's values. And when she receives friend requests from her mum, dad, her older brother and sisters, and even Grandma, she accepts them all. Sarah is wrapped in a set of values that guide, influence and protect her, in both her 'worlds'.

When Sarah wanted Facebook at age 12, her father didn't simply dismiss her request as meaningless or without merit. He saw it as an opportunity to express the values of the family. He took the time to explain why she couldn't have Facebook yet. Family values will help protect children when parents are not with them and, most importantly, help to empower them.

Often when I go into primary schools I ask students a set of questions including, 'How many of you play online games that are rated for older players than you? And who do you play the games with?' In the

A harmless act of telling a small lie about one's age on Facebook can have serious consequences. Consider this fictitious scenario:

An eleven-year-old girl approaches her mum and asks for a Facebook account. Mum knows she should be 13 to be accepted to open one. Mum tells her to just make up a date of birth to make her 13, so she will be accepted. What harm is there? All her mates have done it. The girl adds three years to her age just to be sure, making her 14. She builds up a large number of 'friends', including her mum. She's eventually requested by a friend of a friend, when she actually is 14. This is an 18-year-old guy. He charms her; she agrees to meet him offline; he is the 'man of her dreams'; soon afterwards they have consensual sexual intercourse. Mum finds out and reports the matter to the police, who investigate the allegation.

Police speak to the 18-year-old male. He readily admits having sexual intercourse with the girl, but states he thought she was 17. The officer asks why he thought this, and he replies, 'Because it says so on her Facebook profile. Look, I have a screenshot to prove it.' If he genuinely thought she was 17 years old, this could possibly offer him a defence in law.

Detective Neil Kitchen,
Child Protection, Nelson

majority of schools, I can find seven-, eight- and nine-year-olds who are playing R18 games with friends, fathers or both. **What will our future become if we marinate children in fictional violent games, games that allow them to make choices such as who to kill and how to kill them, and that promote the myth that these actions have no consequences?**

As I travel from Bluff to Kaitaia delivering cyber-safety education in schools, I am increasingly aware of the inappropriate content young children are being exposed to. I regularly receive calls from school principals, social workers and parents who have discovered a child they know is accessing R18 online games, many of them set in violent and sexualised environments.

These games do not promote well-being in the child, they do not contribute to the child valuing self, others or society, and they do not teach a child to be respectful. **These games are not consistent with the values of a family, quite apart from the fact that it is illegal to knowingly allow a young child to play an R18 game.**

Luke is playing his favourite online game, in which he is able to blow up cars, shoot people, run them over, perform sexual acts with them, hit them and torture them. He sometimes plays the game with his dad or his older brother and when he's at his friend's house. Luke has said that his favourite weapon in the game is a knife because 'he really likes to stab people with it'. Luke is just seven years old.

Daniel is eight and he finds a game on his 19-year-old brother's laptop. His brother Mark lets him use the laptop when he isn't home. Daniel's dad notices him playing a game and decides to check on what his son is up to. He is immediately horrified to see the type of language used in the game, and shocked when he watches his son punch another character in the head, who collapses unconscious on the ground. Daniel then steers his character towards a group of people, running at them and shooting them with a shotgun as they fall to the ground, blood pouring across the pavement.

Daniel's father explains to his son that this is not the sort of game he should be playing. He explains that Daniel is too young, that he is not comfortable with the violence and bad language, and that hurting people, even when it's make-believe, is not nice. Daniel says that his older brother Mark is allowed to play the game, so his father explains that Mark is older and legally allowed to play R18 games.

In this exchange, Daniel's father is expressing the values of the family. He is teaching his child to respect the law, and he is teaching his child that violence, even when fictional, is not something a young child should be exposed to. The messages that Daniel's father is giving his son are messages that will contribute to him developing his own set of core values.

A primary school teacher told me about a seven-year-old student who was asked to write a story and read it to the class. He spent most of the morning crafting the story and then showed his work and illustration to the teacher. The boy had drawn a picture of a man holding a baseball bat. Next to him was a woman pushing what the teacher thought was a trolley. The boy explained that it wasn't a trolley, it was a pram with a baby in it. The man was chasing the woman and 'wanted to bash her on the head with his bat so she would die'.

When asked why he had drawn this, the boy explained that he played this game with his dad. Consider how many hours a seven-year-old child could potentially spend playing R18 games before they actually reach the legal age, if this behaviour is allowed. How might that repeated exposure affect their well-being and their view of the world?

In stopping his son from playing an R18 game, Daniel's father was exercising his duty of care. He was protecting his young son's impressionable mind and supporting his well-being. He was teaching him to value and respect others. He was anchoring Daniel to the values of the family.

If you have a strong set of positive family values, then you are well on your way to keeping your child safe and giving them the ability to support others also.

CHAPTER 2

CYBER-SEPARATION

Keeping those lines of communication open

The role of us as parent/caregiver is to nurture and protect our offspring as they grow, empowering them to go on to live successful and meaningful lives. If I ask a parent what 'nurture and protect' means for them, I usually get a range of predictable answers: warmth, love, laughter, food, security, sleep, other children to play with, and the presence of responsible adults.

Naturally, the attributes of good parenting almost always begin in the offline world – an environment we can see and feel, with physical distance, light and three dimensions. In this environment, most parents are good at assessing risk. If the aggressive-looking dog gets too close, we pick the infant up and hold them, waiting for the danger to pass. If another child hits our own in the playground, we can calmly intervene.

But when I ask parents how they nurture and protect their child in the online environment, they often struggle to provide answers. They struggle in part because they don't think of the online world as a place that their child *inhabits*. It is not tangible, it is only two-dimensional, and it is not easily shared. And yet **the online world is equally an environment where your child lives and plays, laughs, cries, learns, communicates and forms friendships, and it is essential that the modern parent understands this,** for without this insight the risk of cyber-separation becomes very real.

Cyber-separation is the disconnection that develops between the child and their parent when the parent has little understanding of or involvement in their child's online world. It is the consequence of unsupervised and independent use of digital communication technology, and it means that the parental protection and oversight generally available to a child offline is absent when the child engages in their online world.

I have seen a worrying increase in the number of children and young people with disturbing behaviours and mental health problems due to excessive time on media (with lack of parenting and supervision). Many schools, medical practices and Child Youth and Family are regularly reporting about primary school children displaying overtly sexualised behaviours impacting on them and other children around them. More often than not, the main factor has been unlimited access to adult games or pornography via the internet. This can be in the background of general neglect, with parents using the tablet or game as a way of avoiding their parental role, but in many cases parents are simply unaware of the inherent dangers of unsupervised internet use.

Dr Giles Bates,
Consultant Paediatrician, MidCentral Health

With cyber-separation, the risk of harm increases as the technology they use becomes more and more sophisticated and parents become more and more distant. The greater the lack of support, knowledge, supervision and involvement that a parent provides a child when they are online, the greater the potential for separation between the child and their parent.

Prolonged cyber-separation from a young age disconnects the child from the beneficial effects of strong family values. A barrier forms between their offline and online worlds, and this can impact severely on a parent's ability to create an open line of communication with their child into this part of their life. This is particularly serious when a child's online world becomes more important to them than the one they have with their parents, which is distressingly common.

Adolescence is also a vulnerable time for children in the digital world, and it is crucial that communication is maintained with your child during this period. Allowing cyber-separation to form can make it harder for parents to assess the risks for their child through these teenage years.

Here is a scenario of how cyber-separation can develop and play out, based on real-life experiences:

From age three Connor plays every day on his mum's iPad and he is getting good at navigating the pages. This allows her to get jobs done, which she is happy about, and Connor is safe, occupied, and she knows exactly where he is. Connor loves playing on the iPad.

By age five Connor is playing computer games regularly. He's now able to download his favourite games, himself. Connor's parents never look at the games their son likes to play but they are really pleased with how focused and occupied he is. They can get on and do what they need to do, and they no longer have his constant declarations that he's bored.

Connor, aged seven, is playing his new online game, in which he is able to blow up cars, shoot people and hit them. He sometimes plays the game with his older brother and when he's at his friend's house.

Connor is now nine years old. One day at school he starts calling girls in the playground 'whores', and asks them to play a game where they sit on the ground while he pretends to drive past them in his car. When the girls agree to play, he pulls up next to them, gets out and walks up to them to hit them with a pretend baseball bat, actually a cardboard tube he's found in the craft room at school.

Fourteen-year-old Connor is online and he finally plucks up the courage and sends Kate a private message asking her to go out with him. She goes to his school and they get on well. Kate instantly replies 'YES'. Connor is really happy, as he knows she likes him. Later that evening Kate sends Connor a private message asking him to send her a naked picture of himself. At first, he feels reluctant and embarrassed, but then thinks to himself, 'What's the problem – everyone does it.' Before sending the picture, he asks Kate for her mobile number as he doesn't want to send the photo online. She sends it and he sends the naked picture.

The next day on the way to school Connor notices a group of students laughing at him. One of the boys, Kate's brother, comes up to him and shows him a picture on his phone. It's the naked picture he sent Kate last night. Kate's brother then admits to Connor that he wasn't talking to Kate last night, but to *him* – she had been out and he had taken over her social network. Connor is horrified, and feels sick and anxious.

The bullying starts after this, with relentless and horrible text messages sent day after day to Connor. Many students are posting upsetting messages to his social network, and at school it is even worse. It seems like everybody hates him, and his naked picture appears to be on everyone's phone. Connor feels lonely, ashamed, and he can't sleep ... he just doesn't want to carry on.

Connor is now 18 and is trying to get his first job, as he wants to take a gap year before going off to university to study law. He is about to be interviewed. This will be his fourth job interview in the last six months. He has applied to do part-time work at a local law firm, applied for a temporary position at a sports club, and sent his CV to eight businesses in the community. Nobody, however, has even replied to his applications, and he hopes that this time he will be successful.

Today he is sitting with three others waiting to be interviewed for a position as a teacher aide at the school he used to attend. In his office, the principal is looking at the information he has available on Connor. His academic ability is obviously good, his CV is professionally put together, and it is quite clear that he is a bright young man. There is a problem, however – Connor's exposure on the internet.

The Board of Trustees has directed the principal to check the background of all potential applicants for positions in the school and to use the internet to vet and filter all applicants. When the principal starts his background search he is shocked. None of what comes up about Connor is illegal – in fact, some show acceptable images of him with his friends and family at barbecues and so on, and without the negative content, may even have helped him secure the position he is applying for – but other images show a side of him that no CV would ever reveal: numerous images of Connor drinking alcohol with friends in nightclubs and various other locations. One of the images shows him vomiting into a gutter. Two of the images have supporting text that is derogatory and insulting to women. Some of the posts have obscene language in them, including derogatory comments about teachers at the very school at which he is applying for a job. The principal has seen enough. He places the internet profile in the drawer, and waits for Connor to enter. Unfortunately, it's likely he won't actually tell Connor the truth about why he's not being considered for the job.

Net-burn

'Net-burn' is the term used to describe the painful effect of over-exposure in cyberspace of a person's personal life, and it is what happened to Connor. Net-burn occurs when a person, young or old, uses the internet without concern for the impact, recording their personal life by posting images and other content on social media, blog sites, chatrooms and any other environment that stores digital content via or on the internet. The result is a large digital footprint that can have a negative impact both emotionally on the person and on the opportunities available to them.

Avoiding cyber-separation is a significant step in ensuring that your child is not burdened by net-burn later in life. Because of their cyber-separation, no opportunity existed for Connor's parents to offer support and guidance as his use of digital communication evolved. The family values that were triggered every time he made a decision or even a mistake in the offline world could not support him online, because these values had not been transferred.

I regularly get to see first-hand how net-burn reduces the opportunity for young people to get the job they want. Most employers today do some type of background check. They will trawl the internet looking for any information a prospective employee or their associates have uploaded about them. **Your child's CV today is a combination of the one they submit to the employer and information available about them online**.

I met a mother and father at a parent workshop who showed me screen shots of their daughter's Facebook and Instagram accounts. The photos showed the girl drinking alcohol from a yard glass, in what appeared to be a bath, half-naked, with two other girls drinking vodka, and a selfie she had posted with related text describing her hatred for her ex-boyfriend's new girlfriend.

Their daughter was now 21 and had spent the last few years at university studying architecture. She was in her final year and wanting to get some part-time work with a firm. Despite her top grades, sending her CV to numerous architectural firms had not come up with any positions. Eventually her father looked into why she was unable to get work. He had a contact in one of the firms his daughter had applied to and asked this person if she could explain his daughter's rejection. The contact's reply: 'This is not official, but take a look at your daughter's digital footprint and ask yourself if you would employ her without any personal knowledge.' The parents checked it out and were shocked and upset.

In partnership with your school

One common contribution to cyber-separation in families is when parents absolve too much responsibility for their child's online well-being and leave it up to their child's school. This is despite the fact that your child will only spend **11 per cent of their time at school in any given year.**

When a child starts school I always advise parents to think carefully about the nature of the relationship they have with the school. It is my belief, and indeed of most teachers, that this should be a partnership, by definition **a shared responsibility**. The more that parents are willing to sign up to this shared responsibility, the better off their child will be. Being in partnership with your child's school plays an important role in how your child responds to the school environment, both offline and online.

In many of the primary schools I work with, I often notice that by late morning some students are struggling to stay awake and are unable to concentrate. Teachers tell me this is a constant issue, and when I ask these students what time they went to bed, it is not uncommon to find out it is as late as 1 a.m. If I ask them whether they were on computers or mobile phones at this time, many of them admit to this, as well as to the fact they turn their devices back on and use them when their parents/caregivers are asleep. This is the worst kind of cyber-separation because the guardians have no knowledge that their young children are even on devices.

Not only will lack of sleep reduce your child's learning capacity at school, but covert use of digital technology is potentially dangerous, as children can be communicating with anybody on the planet. The easiest way to prevent this is to keep technology out of the bedroom. Make sure your child gets enough sleep to cope with the demands of school, and if you establish these rules at a young age it becomes easier to maintain once they start high school.

When working with parents and school students who have managed to get themselves in strife online, and where it involves their school in

> *My mum and dad had gone to bed. I couldn't sleep so I sneaked into the lounge, got my iPad, got back into bed and went online and started playing my favourite game. Somebody in the game dared me to click on a link he had posted, so I did. A new page opened up and what I saw really scared me. I burst into tears and ran into my mum and dad's bedroom. I saw pictures of people hurting animals. I never told them what happened because I shouldn't have been on my device when they are asleep. I told them I'd had a bad dream.*
> **Eight-year-old boy, Nelson**

some way, it is not uncommon to see parents abdicating responsibility for their child's online behaviour, passing that responsibility on to the school.

Kayla, an 11-year-old girl, was being bullied via Facebook by Oliver, one of her classmates. The bullying was also occurring at school in the form of nasty comments in the classroom. One day when the teacher heard Oliver verbally abuse Kayla, he pulled him aside and explained that this was not acceptable behaviour, and Oliver was asked to apologise.

Further investigation by the teacher revealed that Kayla, who by this time was sobbing, had been enduring a mix of online and classroom bullying for four weeks. The principal subsequently got involved, and arranged a meeting with Oliver's parents. When they saw the threatening nature of their son's messages on Facebook, they were horrified.

The principal also met with Kayla's parents, and they, too, were shocked and wanted to find reasons as to why this had happened. Kayla's father asked what the school was going to do to ensure this didn't happen again, and made it clear he held the school responsible for his daughter's well-being whilst in their care.

> *When I hear my mum or dad walking towards my bedroom
> I put my iPad under my sheets and pretend to be asleep.
> Gets them every time.*
> **Twelve-year-old boy, Auckland**

And indeed schools do have a responsibility under the National Administrative Guideline Number 5 (NAG 5) 'to create a safe physical and emotional environment for students'. The principal immediately committed to ensuring that Kayla's teachers would keep a close eye on her, would make sure the school's counsellor was available for Kayla, and would review the school's internal procedures in dealing with Oliver. However, while the principal accepted that when at school they were responsible for Kayla's safety, he also wanted to know from her parents what *they* were going to do to increase her safety and well-being when she was not at school. When Kayla's parents looked confused at this question, the principal pointed out that the online bullying was occurring during the weekends and after school. His further questioning also revealed that Kayla's parents had no idea who she was connected to on Facebook, and that they had let her set up a Facebook account at the age of 11, when the minimum age is 13.

If Kayla's parents had been in touch with her online world, they would have been aware of the bullying and could have reacted appropriately to support and safeguard their daughter. This would have included involving the school, who could then hold Oliver accountable for his actions. Oliver's parents should also have provided more support and supervision for their child at home, and thus the school could provide support to change his behaviour within their environment.

Avoiding cyber-separation begins at home, and it is crucial that parents work in partnership with their child's school if any issues within the online world occur.

It should be noted that schools are often highly regulated environments, whereas most homes are not. For example, schools are required by law to provide a safe environment and will have network filtering in place. In addition, schools will have education programmes, which will often involve outside expertise, as well as policies/procedures for how to handle issues as and when they arise.

As a former principal and now a consultant to schools, my advice to parents is to be active participants in their son/daughter's online life at home as well as when he or she is at school. Too often I see parents, whose child has done or seen something online while at school that isn't appropriate, blame the school.

If that child has a strong set of family values to draw on, in addition to the skills and values the school will teach, then he/she is set up to be an effective citizen for the 21st century. Schools cannot do this work alone.

Rob Clarke,
Educational Leadership Consultant, Learning Architects

STRATEGIES FOR PARENTS
How to reduce cyber-separation between yourself and your child

- Try to always maintain open lines of communication with your child. Do not overreact if you see something that alarms you or makes you angry. Share your concerns, and always talk about issues in terms of how they relate to your child and their friends' safety.

- Don't let your child store or use their devices in the bedroom when they are young. If you establish a 'not in the bedroom' rule it will help to avoid conflict and issues when they are older.

- In the same way we are excited about them learning to ride a bicycle, show enthusiasm and interest when they use any form of technology. Showing interest will promote open communication between you and your child.

- Become your child's 'friend' in any social network environment your child creates.

- Maintain easy access to your child's platform via their log-in. This means that you will see everything.

- Ensure that you can always have access to your child's phone to help them stay safe. When the phone is first purchased, make sure that this is a condition of them having it, and never let it become a no-go area. Always check the quality of how they are communicating with others and that it is consistent with the values of your family.

- Educate your child about the importance of protecting family and friends' images. Teach them to seek permission before they send or upload images of anyone else to the internet.

- Encourage your child that if somebody asks them to remove a picture of themselves they don't like or want uploaded, respect the person and remove it.

- Agree on a time in the evening when everybody stops using technology within the home. This becomes family time. It's important to note that how we work and when we work has changed beyond all recognition, much of it due to technology. The lines between work and home are increasingly blurred. It is vital that we put boundaries around our work to allow our family to share time and space together. Respect our child's need to have time with us. Give them time to talk, listen to them and be with them. The most important relationship you have is the one with your child, not the one with your computer or mobile phone.

- You are not their friend; you are their guardian. Have clear guidelines in place and consequences when rules are broken around the use of digital technology.

- Check that your child knows all of the people in their social networks. If not, ask that they delete them.

- Remember your child is introduced to technology the first time they see *you* use it. If you don't put your device down when your child comes to you to talk, they won't put their device down when you want to make eye contact with them.

- If your child does make a mistake, a poor choice or finds themselves connected to a situation that is not in harmony with your family values, do not overreact. It is vital that you keep the lines of communication open with your child. Tell your child that no matter what they do you will always love them and be there for them, because nothing can break this bond. This will help build an open, non-judgemental relationship that is vital as your child becomes a teenager.

- From time to time check on what applications they have downloaded. If you don't recognise it, check it out by trying theirs or you could get them to demonstrate it to you.

- When you're checking the applications, ask yourself if they're consistent with your family values. If not, consider deleting them.

- Occasionally check your child's browser history. Doing this will allow you to see the websites and information they have been accessing. You can use Google to find out where this is or ask your local IT provider. It is a very quick, simple process.

- Make sure older children model safe use of technology around their younger siblings as this will have a significant influence on how the younger ones interact with the online world.

- Teach older members of your family not to expose younger members to games or content that is inappropriate for their age or level of maturity.

- Use monitoring and filtering software for younger members of your family. This allows you to control your child's use of a computer by restricting access to specific websites and placing time limits on their use. The software can also allow you to block access to internet content you consider unsuitable for your child to view.

- If new friends are introduced online, encourage your child to be open about who they are and what they are up to. When in doubt, call the parents and introduce yourself.

- Paedophiles gravitate to areas where children play, communicate and congregate, so you must pay attention to the online games your children play and make sure they are consistent with the values of your family. Questions to ask include:
  - Is the game age-appropriate?
  - Is the quality of the language suitable for a child?
  - How does the game make money out of a child's use?
  - What processes are available to adults should they need to make a complaint about a user?
- If you're also learning about how digital communication technology works, pick some areas that you don't know about and ask your child to teach you. You'll not only be interacting with your child but also building a relationship that reduces cyber-separation.
- When you give a child any type of digital device you should teach them how to take screen shots on that device. This is easy to learn – use Google.
- If a child shuts down a computer when you enter the room, leaves the room to talk on the phone in private, refuses to let you see who is sending messages or won't let you near any of their devices, regard this as a serious warning sign that something could be wrong. It is very important that secrecy is not normalised. **Nosy parents are loving parents, and the nosier you are, the more you love your children.**
- Allow your child to have access to social networks and games at the correct age, and not before. Doing this not only keeps them safe but also teaches them respect for the companies' products they are using.
- When they create online social networks make sure their first friend requests are from you and other family members. This includes any application that allows them to broadcast or receive content. This wraps the child in the family values and will reduce the effects of cyber-separation.

CHAPTER 3

A DIGITAL BOUNDARY

Making informed, ethical decisions

One of the most important tools I use to teach young people how to keep safe online is the concept of a digital boundary. With five- to seven-year-olds, I use the term 'safe circle', and ask them to be 'cybernauts', who are trained to go into cyberspace and take care of themselves, their family and their friends.

Understanding and developing a digital boundary teaches children to broadcast decent and positive values across the internet. If we can give children and young people the ability to learn how to make informed, ethical decisions online, founded on common decency and reasonable standards of right and wrong, it will significantly reduce the chances for harm to occur to themselves, their family and friends.

Advice for parents of younger children about creating a safe circle

- When taking pictures of your children, ask their permission. Then turn the camera around and ask them if they like the picture or not. If they don't, offer to delete it. The sooner we give children the right to control their own identity the sooner we will 'power them up' to protect it.

- When you go to weddings, barbecues and other family events, give your child your phone/camera and let them be the official photographer at the party. Teach them to ask permission of the guests before taking the picture. This will show your child from a young age that someone's identity is important.

- Teach your children not to post pictures online of themselves sitting in their bedroom. Their bedroom is their private sanctuary, a place to

My mum told me off for taking a picture of her in her jammas and putting it on Instagram without asking her first. She has been doing that with pictures of me from the day I was born. I still love you, mum.
Eleven-year-old girl, Gisborne

feel safe. If it is exposed online, it reduces their ability to *conceptually* build the safe circle that wraps around them.

- Teach them never to ignore their 'butterflies' and their gut feelings. When they do get butterflies, let them know the butterflies are their friends trying to help them. Teach them in these moments to take a deep breath and tell you what is worrying them.

- Teach them that a cybernaut never responds to people online who are being mean and that when they don't reply, they have all the power. Get them to show you their power by doing the power pose: chin up and shoulders back.

- Teach them if they see something on a computer that upsets them or worries them to simply close the lid or just look away from the screen and come and tell you. Let them know you will give them a big hug for being a really smart cybernaut.

- If you see your child about to play an online game, ask them, 'Where are you going?' This will help them think about cyberspace as a place they are going *to*, not one that comes to them.

- Don't let your child surf the internet indiscriminately. Just as we don't want young people visiting certain locations in towns or cities, we should regard the internet in the same way. Paedophiles use specific techniques to attract minors to them. Get your child to think about creating a road map before they go online. Ask them to tell you who or what they are visiting.

When your child starts to engage with digital technology more, look for opportunities to pass on advice that will keep them technically safe. Here are three examples:

- When you give them a digital device or their first online game to play, teach them the importance of passwords and why they should use them to protect their information and keep it inside their safe circle.

- Teach them about not sharing these with other people, in the same way we don't give the keys to our house to a stranger.

- As they start to use more and more devices and applications, help them to create different passwords for each device.

Digital Boundary: Family/Friends/Self

As a child grows, they develop a natural boundary between safe and unsafe behaviour. This is modelled by their parents and the culture they are raised in, and plays a major role in protecting them in everyday life. This boundary also needs to become a fundamental reference point when they engage and make decisions in the digital online world.

For example, a teenager at a party takes an inappropriate photo of a friend and posts it online. It is then seen by her mother because they share the same social network. The mother is upset, but her daughter considers her to be overreacting; a common dynamic. However, because their family has an agreed set of standards, and a boundary not based on risk or harm but on respect and family values, the mother and her daughter have a reference point from which they can debate the choices her daughter has made.

It is important to reiterate the difference between your child learning the *technical skills* that improve security online, what I call 'functional competency', and learning to create a *digital boundary*, which allows your child to make decisions that contribute to their personal safety and psychological well-being, including that of their family and friends.

The foundation of any digital boundary is family values

Imagine if you had only one of two ways to help your child stay safe online:

1. You could teach your child how to use the security controls on social networks, such as Facebook and the numerous online gaming platforms they use, to help reduce the risk of harm. You could also teach them how to keep their passwords safe and to not give them out to friends.

2. You could regularly reinforce your family values with your child, giving them a strong sense of self-worth, developing their resilience and always reminding them that they are unique and priceless.

Which one would you choose?

The first option provides a limited measure of safety, specific to each platform or device. The second option empowers your child, preparing them for life both online and offline. And, importantly, it provides them with the motivation to keep secure any online environment with which they engage.

Functional competency is easy to learn. You can teach a young person to drive a car within a few hours. But teaching them to respect road rules, other drivers and pedestrians is based on values and is an essential aspect of being a safe and responsible driver.

Focusing too much on functional competency and not enough on self-respect and respect for others leaves a child less motivated to seek out the boundaries for themselves.

The key task for any child or young person is to understand that there are three elements they must keep safe inside their own digital boundary. These are:

- family
- friends
- self

Here is a range of examples of digital boundaries to keep children and young people safe:

Protecting a friend

A teenage girl has been out at a party. When she comes home she finds a photo on her phone she took earlier of her friend lying on a couch drinking alcohol. In the background of the photo she notices a boy who is being disrespectful to the girl, with inappropriate hand gestures. She decides not to upload the picture, and instead deletes it. The girl has kept her friend inside of her digital boundary and she is reflecting her family values by demonstrating respect.

Managing your personal safety

A 12-year-old boy is playing an online game on a multi-level server, which means he can play the game with people he has only met online. While playing it, somebody asks him 'What school do you go to?' The boy does not answer the question. He knows he should not disclose anything unrelated to the game, and he has kept himself inside his digital boundary.

Demonstrating respect and valuing your friends

A boy wants to take a photo of his friend. He asks his friend's permission. If the boy agrees and he takes the photo, he has kept his friend inside his digital boundary by seeking permission. If the boy says no and he therefore doesn't take the photo, he has also kept his friend inside his digital boundary.

Promoting your family's safety

Scarlet is 13 and has 44 people connected to her online social network. A friend request comes in from a boy who looks nice. But because she doesn't know him, Scarlet declines the request. She knows that if she lets a stranger inside her digital boundary, that stranger can see who her friends are and learn about their lives. Scarlet also knows of homes that have been burgled by criminals who watch what people talk about online.

Protecting your friends and yourself

Lucas is playing an online game with his friend Jake and six other boys from school. There are also lots of other players he doesn't know. The game is going really well until Ethan, a boy he knows from school, comes into the game. Ethan doesn't like Jake and has been bullying him at school for the last six weeks, using nasty low-level comments which have really upset Jake. Lucas has noticed how he is becoming withdrawn. With Ethan's encouragement, other boys join in online and start harassing Jake.

Lucas's first instinct is to defend his friend online, but he realises that this is just giving power to the bullies. So Lucas takes screen shots of the bullying comments. He then texts Jake, encouraging him to leave the game and reassures him that he will help get the bullying stopped.

Lucas is protecting his friend by taking the screen shots, which will become evidence they can show parents, teachers or even the police, and he has controlled his urge to strike back at the bullies.

Looking after yourself

Niko is eight, and every Tuesday after school he goes to his friend John's house for a sleepover. For the last three weeks, just before going to bed, John and Niko have played a game that Niko had heard about but never played before. He knows enough to know he shouldn't play it because he is too young. John was given the game by his uncle, despite the fact that it is R18. The game is extremely realistic, with high-definition graphics, copious amounts of blood and loud screaming.

Niko starts having bad dreams, many of which are similar to the game he plays with John. One afternoon his mum picks him up from school and notices he looks tired and stressed. When she asks what is wrong, Niko bursts into tears and confesses how guilty he feels for playing a game he knows she wouldn't want him to play. As Niko is able to tell his mum what has happened, he manages to re-establish his digital boundary. By doing so he is successfully managing himself and respecting his family values.

STRATEGIES FOR PARENTS

How to build a digital boundary

....

- Depending on the age of your child, they could read this book for themselves or you could read and discuss with them what a digital boundary is.

- Remember to ensure that your child's online life is consistent with your family values, and that they do actually accept the safety measures in place. Talk about how their behaviour online affects you and other family members, and that it is a shared responsibility.

- Do not fall into the trap of excessively restricting your child's access to the online world, especially if it is simply because you don't like the technology or are of a nervous disposition – this simply increases the risk of cyber-separation. Modelling anxiety when talking to your child about safety can increase the risk of your child becoming anxious when they engage with technology.

- Encourage them to use digital technology, be excited for them (fake it if you have to). When it's time for them to have a mobile phone, treat it like a special event.

A DIGITAL BOUNDARY CONTRACT

☐ I need to maintain a digital boundary when online, where I will keep my family, friends and myself safe.

☐ I am unique and there is only one of me on the planet. My identity belongs to me, and I will protect it and nurture it. This is the same for my family's and friends' identities.

☐ Before taking a picture of one of my friends or family members I will always seek permission.

☐ I will not allow people to take pictures of me that are inappropriate or inconsistent with my family values.

☐ When communicating with people I have only met online, such as in an online game in cyberspace or when using an application installed on my mobile phone that allows me to communicate, I will always do my best to leave out personal information.

☐ I will never go and meet people I have met online in the physical world, unless a parent or adult is present. I will NEVER break this rule. It is non-negotiable.

☐ When playing online games that require images I will use an avatar (or mask) and create an internet name. The name will not be my real name and it will be consistent with the values of my family.

☐ I will not ignore my gut feelings. If something bothers me when communicating with someone online, I will talk to someone I trust, such as my parents or my Lighthouse (see chapter 5 for explanation).

☐ When I use any form of digital communication I will learn how to use functions and security settings to help keep myself and others safe. I will take the time to demonstrate to my parents that I am functionally competent and not use the application, social network or online game until I can demonstrate this skill.

☐ I will only use online games, chatrooms, visit websites and install applications on my devices that are consistent with my family values.

☐ If anybody online talks to me and tries to pressure me for personal information, I will stop communicating with them and take control of the situation. I will tell an adult I trust what has happened.

☐ I will never accept a gift from a stranger online or offline. Paedophiles sometimes send gifts to children as part of the 'grooming' process. If anybody I have met online wants to send me a gift, I will inform my parents or an adult I can trust without delay.

☐ If a person asks me to keep a secret, I will remember that this is a warning sign I could be in danger. Paedophiles rely on secrecy and don't want me to talk to parents or others about them.

☐ When I'm on the internet, I will not follow links or leave one online location and follow a person to another location. For example, if I am playing an online game and someone asks me to go to another chatroom or asks to talk on Skype or a similar video-streaming platform, this is a warning sign and I will stop communicating and talk to an adult.

CHAPTER 4

CYBER-MUSCLES

A chin-up, shoulders-back attitude online

....

When I am presenting workshops to students I ask them to tell me who comes to mind when they think of a person who has power and control. The answers often include sports people, especially the All Blacks, standing in front of their opponents just before kickoff, chins up, shoulders back, projecting power and control. Or Valerie Adams, and how she projects control when she is competing in shot-put, and projecting respect, self-control and humility off the sports field.

Learning to project confidence, power and control is a very useful life skill, as it lets other people know the kind of person they are dealing with and how that person is likely to react in certain situations. Projecting this type of body language helps protect us.

If a person on holiday in New York City is walking down the street looking confused and anxious, constantly checking a map or looking at their phone, they are at an increased risk of being mugged by somebody who is observing their body language of being lost. And of the thousands of people who will pass them by, they are unaware of who is the potential attacker.

But, if they could lift their head up, tilt their chin back, take long, confident strides and only look at their map or phone in a private space, they decrease the risk of being mugged and of standing out and looking lost.

Just as you can learn in the physical world how to project a chin-up, shoulders-back attitude, it is an equally important skill for children and young people to learn online. Because just like a tourist walking down the street in New York, your child never knows who could be observing them online.

We can help our children project power and control online by developing their 'cyber-muscles': the skills that allow your child to broadcast confidence when using digital communication technology.

A powered-up child

When a child knows how to protect themselves if things get out of control, when they know how to react and how to get help when needed, this child is powered up. The child understands that what they communicate online in image or text only works when it is in harmony with their family values. The child understands that their identity belongs to them, they own it and they control it. A child who is powered up shows empathy, is compassionate and anchored to their family's values.

A child who has cyber-muscles will be **capable, confident** and **connected**.

Being **capable** means using family values to broadcast their self-worth.

Being **confident** means using a digital boundary to make safe, ethical decisions.

Being **connected** means understanding how to use security settings in online applications to stay safe, and being willing to seek support from adults if things go wrong.

Jacob, an 11-year-old boy, is registering to play an online game, a game in which other children he doesn't know can interact with him. He is required to upload a picture of himself and provide his name. This will then be seen by other players in the game.

Jacob recalls how his parents are always saying to him, 'There is only one of you on the planet, you are unique, you are precious and we love you, so protect your identity. You own it and it belongs to nobody else.' Therefore, instead of a picture of himself he creates an avatar, or a mask (I prefer the term 'mask' because it describes its purpose). He also gives himself an internet name, calling himself 'Ninja'. He is demonstrating **capability**.

As he enters the game he sees that ten other players are already in the game. Nine are children, some with masks and some without, but the tenth person is actually an adult male. This man likes to observe children in online games to see what they talk about and how they react to certain questions. The adult notices Ninja enter the game; he also notices he has created a mask to protect his identity.

A child in the game says 'Hi' to Ninja and Ninja replies with a 'Hi'. Another player asks Ninja how old he is but Ninja doesn't reply. Another player asks Ninja what his real name is, but he makes it clear he only gives out his internet name when online.

The adult can see that Ninja, aka Jacob, is projecting power and control. By being prepared before he even enters the game or says anything, Jacob is projecting power. He has a mask and an internet name. He does not discuss personal things and he isn't afraid to say no. He is using his cyber-muscles and is demonstrating **confidence**.

At one point in the game two players start to verbally attack Ninja, saying nasty things about his skill level. Ninja does not reply, but simply blocks the players and reports them to the game operators via the Block and Report functionality available to users of the game. He also takes screen shots to gather evidence, which he then shows his parents. He stays in control of himself, he has power over them and himself, and he is demonstrating that he is **connected**.

Just like the tourist walking down the street in New York, Jacob had no idea he was being observed by an adult in the game, but he was projecting the right attitude, with chin up and shoulders back. He was showing that he was confident and in control, not only over the technology but also over his own behaviour.

Nine-year-old Hannah is playing on the beach with her younger brother, while her parents are a few metres away enjoying the warm weather and watching over the family. Three tourists walking past stop and take pictures of the children playing. Hannah looks to her parents for guidance because she doesn't like it – it feels intrusive and creepy. The parents look at each other, unsure as to how to respond, then her mum just smiles awkwardly, waiting for the moment to pass. The tourists finish taking the photo and move on. Hannah's parents have just taught the children to be socially compliant with strangers even when *they* don't want to be. We need to teach our children to be respectful but not socially compliant to strangers when it doesn't feel right, both in the physical world and in the online world.

Tourists taking photos are not usually being malicious, and their motivation is capturing what is new and interesting in a foreign country. However, **if we want children to become resilient, and have power and control over their own identity, we must model how to achieve this when we are presented with opportunities to do so.**

When Hannah looked to her mum and dad for guidance and support, their reaction only reinforced in her mind that it is best to 'suck it up' and wait till it's stopped. How might that affect Hannah later in life? What happens when she is 15 and a partner asks her to send him an inappropriate photograph, which she doesn't want to send?

Powering up a child begins at a young age. If Hannah's parents had smiled politely at the tourists and said 'no', or put up a hand gesturing them to stop, they would have modelled to their children that we own our identity, we control it and we have a right to protect it.

Teach your children they have the right to say no.

Target-hardening

'Target-hardening' is a term associated with security and the military, and describes a place or location that has taken deliberate steps to protect itself from an attack. I use this term in the context of keeping children safe online because I think it is an important concept for young people to grasp – they need to ensure that they are not an easy target for anyone with bad intentions.

We need our children and young people to be target-hardened, and developing their cyber-muscles is one of the most effective ways they can achieve this. A young person who projects power and confidence, and understands the practical security steps to take when online is far less likely to be a target.

> *John, I did what you said. I was a playing a game with four boys from school and two from another school. Two started being mean to me. I stopped communicating with them, grabbed my screen shots, put them in a folder and showed dad. He said he was proud of me. My dad contacted their mum and dad and showed them. I love my cyber muscles.*
> **Nine-year-old girl, Queenstown**

STRATEGIES FOR PARENTS

Developing your child's cyber-muscles

- Regularly reinforce the concepts of being capable, confident and connected when online, as the essential foundations of building cyber-muscles.

- Teach your child to be sensitive to red flags and warning signs when online, to avoid potentially dangerous situations. Encourage them to always listen to their gut feelings, and not ignore them. If it doesn't feel right it probably isn't, and if they are exposed to content that is inconsistent with your family values then they should have the confidence to remove themselves from the situation.

- Use scene-setting with your child to teach them how to use their cyber-muscles. Create imaginary situations and ask them to outline what they would do, and how they would stay safe. This will highlight if the young person has the appropriate level of knowledge, and it creates a safe environment for your child to practise what to do in a threatening situation.

- Teach your child about the concept of repelling unwanted attention. Repelling includes not responding to a person who asks inappropriate questions, or not responding when a person harasses them online. Reinforce that when they don't respond, they take control of the situation and are projecting power and control. As well as repelling, encourage them to always report these incidents to an appropriate adult, and to gather evidence with screen shots if necessary.

- From a young age teach your children that it is OK to say no to strangers who want or try to take photos of them. They can do this verbally or by holding up their hands. Practise this with them by doing scene-setting or role plays.

- Teach your child that it's good to say sorry if they offend somebody online or off. We all make mistakes but an apology can help show who we really are.

CHAPTER 5

COMMUNICATION AND THE 'CYBER-TOOTH TIGER'

Keep it in its cage

One of the big challenges I face when trying to keep children and young people safe online is maintaining positive communication between young people and their parents when things go wrong.

I've worked with young people who have endured severe bullying for months but who did not feel they could talk to their parents about the situation for fear of being shouted at, and/or losing their device. There was one teenage boy who could not bring himself to tell his father about a poor choice he had made. Some weeks earlier he had sent a picture of himself to a girl he really liked, portraying himself in a sexual pose. The girl lost her phone, another student found it, saw the image and distributed the image to other students at the school. The boy was then subjected to endless bullying both in person and online.

When I asked him why he couldn't tell his parents, he recalled watching a documentary on TV with his father about teenagers who were being blackmailed after sending sexy pictures of themselves to people they believed were going to become girlfriends. In reality, the boys were being enticed by young girls promising romance at a later date, but who were actually being used by an organised crime gang. At the conclusion of the documentary, the boy's father had commented that 'those boys are stupid and deserve everything they get'. After getting himself into his own situation, he couldn't bring himself to tell his father. Eventually we were able to get support for the boy via his school guidance counsellor.

Tame your cyber-tooth tiger

I use the term 'cyber-tooth tiger' to describe the parent/caregiver who overreacts when they learn that their child is in trouble or danger because they've either made a mistake or a poor choice online, or somebody else has made a mistake or poor choice online that has affected them. When a parent's cyber-tooth tiger emerges, they tend to shout and scream, accuse their child of being stupid, and use the classic 'What is wrong with you?' line. I have come across many examples of this.

A young boy in an online game is asked inappropriate questions by a potential paedophile. The boy reacts responsibly by not replying to the paedophile, leaves the game and tells his father what has happened. He has kept himself inside his digital boundary, flexed his cyber-muscles and reported the incident to his father.

The father reacts by taking the game off the boy and telling him he can no longer play the game, that 'computers are dangerous and he's sick of them in the house'. The father has let his cyber-tooth tiger out of the cage, and his overreaction is likely to encourage cyber-separation between his son and himself. If the boy is presented with a threat online in the future, unfortunately there is little incentive for him to report this to his father.

A parent or caregiver reacting to immediate danger is highly instinctive and has evolved from the days when sabre-tooth tigers really were prowling around the campfire. I do always remind young people

> *I was on my dad's computer playing a game. I clicked on a link that told me I'd won a prize. I filled in my name and phone number and clicked the submit button. Suddenly these messages popped up with horrible nude pictures of grownups and I couldn't close them. I shut the computer and went to bed feeling scared. I couldn't tell him – he would really shout at me.*
>
> **Nine-year-old girl, Levin**

I have worked as a consultant paediatrician in community paediatrics, child protection and child and adolescent mental health for nearly two decades. Young people can develop suicidal thoughts or self-harm due to cyber-bullying via Facebook, Twitter, Instagram and other social networks. The young people often lack the awareness or skills on how to deal with the problem and parents can be unaware of the issue until the young person presents acutely to mental health services.

Many families appear to have lost the ability to communicate in a way that enhances close relationships with their child. Few children are being read to at night time and families don't sit together to eat anymore, crucial times for discussions and downloading. Some parents are more interested in their Facebook page than spending quality time with their children.

Schools and mental health services have noticed a rapid rise in emotionally dysregulated children and young people in the last couple of years, associated with a lack of strong family connections to ground the young person.

Dr Giles Bates,
Consultant Paediatrician, MidCentral Health

that a parent or caregiver's overreaction is usually an indication of how much he or she loves them and wants to protect them. The problem remains, however, that letting the tiger loose is usually counter-productive.

During one presentation, with over eight hundred high-school students in a hall, I asked them to tell me what they thought were the greatest barriers a teenager faces when wanting to ask a parent for help when they've got into trouble online.

The responses were all along the lines of, 'We don't want to ask them for help because they freak out and blame us', to 'They take the device off us', while another girl commented, 'It didn't matter who was responsible, and even if it was someone else's fault, they'd start shouting. It's like they blame us for what somebody else has done.'

'How many of you think your parents overreact when things go wrong online, and does this make you hesitate to ask for help?' I then asked them.

It was as if a wave had started at the front of the room and swept up into the far reaches of the hall. At my best estimate, at least five to six hundred teenagers put their hands up. This was a sobering revelation.

It is worth finding out for yourself: does your child fear your cyber-tooth tiger?

We can either support our children when they make a mistake or we can judge them, but we can't do both. Developing open lines of communication is a key factor in them staying safe and behaving ethically, online. **Cyber-separation will develop if parents overreact and make harsh judgements.**

The Lighthouse

Many of the teenagers I've worked with over the last ten years have one thing in common: they've been victims of a crime or were potentially on their way to becoming victims of a crime. Many came from loving backgrounds with supportive parents but who just made poor choices because they were young and human.

No matter how good the communication between a child and their parent, there are occasions when it is simply too hard for the child to talk about a problem. Embarrassment, shame and fear can contribute to the child creating a barrier, as well as a sense that their parent may not be able to cope.

> *I just wished I could have told someone what was happening. I couldn't tell my mum, as she had separated from my dad and had enough to deal with. I needed a place to feel safe, another person to go to.*
>
> **Fourteen-year-old victim of bullying**

I have talked regularly with teenagers who have wished that they had had someone to go to for help before their situation got worse. One 15-year-old boy had been bullied severely by other teenagers because of his homosexuality. He couldn't go to his parents because he had as yet not come out to them. He endured the bullying for months until finally he stopped me outside a school hall and tearfully told me about his pain and anguish. He desperately needed somewhere else to go.

A 12-year-old girl came up to me one day at school and told me that she had sent a naked picture of herself to a boy. She said she felt sick and stressed and couldn't sleep, but she couldn't tell her mum because she was so embarrassed.

What both these young people needed was a person to go to whom they trusted, and who could help them either deal with the situation or ideally start a communication with their parent. This person is an intermediary, a go-between: a Lighthouse. A Lighthouse shows the way to safety, a Lighthouse guides them home, hopefully back to their parents.

Sit down with your child and let them nominate a person they and you trust and who shares the same values as you to become their Lighthouse person. Make this a special moment in both your child's life and for your nominated person.

The role of the Lighthouse is to be there for your child at any time, day or night, in person or by phone, to listen to them and help them when they need it, and then support the child and accompany them to meet their guardians and talk about what has happened. As the parent/caregiver, you can also identify all the support services that are there to help them in their role. And reassure them that in most cases the services are confidential.

When you actively provide this opportunity for a Lighthouse with your child, you build a safe passage for them back to you and give them permission to get help when they might need it.

At these times let your child know how much they mean to you. Take some time to remind them how much you love them, that there is nothing you wouldn't do to help them and you will always be there for them.

The Appendix on page 152 has a list of available organisations and support services.

CHAPTER 6

THE ACCEPTABLE USE OF DIGITAL DEVICES

It's all a matter of balance

It is perhaps one of the most debated and stressful issues for parents in today's world where screens are now everywhere – what is the acceptable amount of daily use on a digital device for a young person?

I was recently asked to work with James, a 12-year-old boy, whose parents claimed was always on his computer, both during the week and over the weekend. They wanted guidance on what strategies they could implement to help control James's use of screen time within the home.

The objective in a situation like this is to create a fair and balanced relationship with digital technology that relates to the entire family, but one that allows them to also relate to each other. I see such a scenario requiring a four-stage process:

1. An assessment of James's use of his computer, under two categories: *education* and *entertainment*. What are the school-related commitments such as reports, projects and assignments to complete, and when are screens being used to relax and have fun?

2. A definition of limits: how much time is required for school commitments and what is an acceptable amount of time for entertainment?

3. A collaborative assessment: how is everyone else in the family using digital devices for their education/work commitments and entertainment?

4. Create a family plan for the overall use of digital devices in the home, split between education, work and entertainment. Then, the

most important part of this plan: identify what opportunities are left over for each member of the family to do other things that don't involve a screen, but do include spending time together.

When I met with James and his family, I watched his body language, as he sat with his arms folded and scowling, while his parents and sister provided me with endless examples of how much time he spent on his computer, sometimes until two in the morning. It was evident he was spending too much time on his screens, and that other aspects of his life were being neglected – school work was not being completed and he was always tired at school. This clearly needed to be addressed.

But I also wanted James to have his say during this meeting, and when I asked him to describe to me the rest of the family's use of digital technology within the home, he noticeably changed: he unfolded his arms and he sat up. James's version of a typical day was that his father got up in the morning, read the news on his iPad over breakfast; after he showered, he took his mobile phone into the bedroom to answer the messages he missed in the bathroom. By the time James had got out of the bathroom, his dad had gone to work.

In the evening his father worked in his office on his computer until 7 p.m. During dinner his dad always had his phone on the table, read his personalised news feed, then would go back to his office and watch the news on TV. At the same time his mum and sister would watch TV in the lounge. At this point, James would go to his room to hook into his computer and play an online game.

After this description of events there was silence in the room, until his mum chipped in with the added observation that James's dad would also play golf from 10 a.m.–4 p.m. every Saturday.

James said that if the family ever did sit down together to watch a film, his dad was always on his phone looking at it or answering work-related text messages, while his sister was constantly on Facebook and Instagram. With his mum running a small business, she would be monitoring Trade Me. James's last comment was, 'We don't really sit and talk much anymore.'

During the family meeting the daughter admitted that she probably spent just as much time on a digital device as her brother, and while she isn't a gamer, she spent hours on Facebook, sitting in the lounge with

> *John, we sat down as a family to have dinner and I pulled*
> *out my phone as a text had just arrived. My eight-year-*
> *old son said, 'Mum, I love you very much. Can you leave*
> *the phone over there so we can all eat together and talk?'*
> *He said you had told his class to say that when they have*
> *family meals or family time. I did what he said and my*
> *husband turned off the TV. Thank you for giving my child a*
> *voice in his home.*
> **Mother, Auckland**

her phone. She suggested that maybe her parents didn't react to her use of her phone in the same way they did to her brother because she was not locked away in her room.

It was also clear that James's dad spent more time on his entertainment needs, both on screen and on the golf course, than his son spent on his. The real issue being overlooked was the lack of actual family time being made available by them.

In my opinion, one of the mistakes in dealing with the issue of acceptable use is that parents try to set time limits on use of screens. While this is crucial when children are young, these boundaries become far harder to define and to adopt when children get older, particularly when they transition into adolescence.

I favour a different approach, which is to **set up times of the day when it is agreed that nobody in the family uses a screen, especially around meal times, morning and night, and when visitors come around**. This needs to be adopted by the whole family with the shared understanding that digital devices are not compatible with family time. The acceptable use of digital technology then becomes a team effort, an issue for the whole family to adopt and enforce.

I often ask high-school students to respond to my questions, and to the one: 'If you approach an adult in your family to ask them a question, for advice or just to have a chat while they are using a screen, do they usually a) continue using the device and talk with you at the same time, or b) stop using the device and talk to you?

Nearly half of the teenagers in that school hall responded with (a).

All children have a right to be noticed by their parents; it is fundamental to a healthy relationship. **Cyber-separation actually works both ways, and it is surprisingly common for a whole family to be consumed by their individual use of digital technology, to the detriment of family time**.

Ask yourself right now, when was the last time you sat down as a family and enjoyed each other's company? If you can say that you did so today, then ask yourself, how often do you create these opportunities in your family? It shouldn't be a rare event.

Lack of sleep

An increasing concern of teachers is how tired many students are at school. On numerous occasions I have asked students what time they think they get to sleep, and to my horror, seven- and eight-year-olds can quite often tell me that bedtime is 10 p.m., 11.30 p.m. and later.

A 12-year-old girl admitted to me, 'When I go to bed I get my tablet out and watch YouTube videos and I just end up staring at the screen, not really watching, just zombing out. I just wish someone would come into the bedroom and take it off me.'

A 14-year-old boy said, 'I hook into my computer till about 2 a.m. most mornings and fall asleep about 3 a.m. By 11 a.m. at school I'm falling asleep. When I get home, I crash out on the sofa for about four hours. Then when I go to bed I find it hard to get to sleep so I get my computer out.'

The child's bedroom today has become a multi-purpose portal for communication and entertainment. It used to be a single-purpose environment. Traditionally the bedroom was a private space where a child could go and relax, to have quiet time. If they'd had a bad day they could shut the door and recharge, and, of most importance, they understood it was a place to sleep. And when they closed that door to shut out the world or go to bed, nothing in the room beeped, nothing in the room radiated light except perhaps the warm glow of a bedside lamp.

Experience and research has shown us that regular, uninterrupted sleep is essential for a young person's health and well-being. It is vital that from an early age no digital devices should be allowed in a young

Evolutionary psychology

If we consider our ancient human history we can recognise some factors that are still important to feeling good and creating balance in our lives. By measuring from early hominids through to present day, some say 98 per cent of our history has been literally as hunter-gatherers. That means daily effort and physical challenges, sunshine and rain, with social engagement in hunting parties or to gather foods, or for protection, procreation, and to cook and eat together.

The sounds we hear, the surroundings we are in, the sensations we experience have all been provided by nature. It also means that when the big light in the sky is out, we sleep, perhaps with exceptions when there is strong moonlight or dangers requiring alertness. When dawn comes there is the natural early wakening along with the rest of creation. With this being our heritage from eons – from millions of years of hunting and gathering – we can validly say that our bodies and our psyches expect these things to occur in some form, every day. We can also say that we leave them out at our peril.

It's notable that when we holiday, we generally like to camp or tramp or fish or surf and play games or sports. Stress goes away to the degree that we give ourselves over to these experiences, which parallel those of the hunter-gatherer. We forget our timetables and may even let go our digital devices. As a consequence sleep patterns turn towards the more satisfying primordial patterns of early to bed, early to rise, and, along with outer activity in natural surroundings, this all fits better with the natural light–dark cycles and rhythms of life which our minds and bodies expect. Well-being readily emerges from such foundations.

Geoffrey Samuels,
Clinical Psychologist

person's bedroom. At the very least if they take them into the bedroom they should be removed at least an hour before the child is meant to be asleep.

Be aware of technology creep

It is my belief that **whatever boundaries we set up in the home are put in place as much to protect the individual as to protect the family structure.** It is vital that families communicate, collaborate and share ideas. Doing things together, whether it's one sister building a chicken coop with her sister or dad cooking dinner with his son, builds deep family bonds and interpersonal intelligence – the ability to understand and interact effectively with others. Digital technology is important in your child's life, but never at the expense of face-to-face communication.

> *I built this wooden cave and ran into the house and asked my dad to look out the window at it. He said in a minute, he was on his iPad. He never looked, John.*
> **Seven-year-old girl, Tauranga**

We need to think of the home like a democracy, and just like a democracy, it requires that we be vigilant to protect it. The minute we stop watching, the minute we stop reminding each other of what is the acceptable use of screens within the home, technology starts to creep in, and we have a family dynamic with an increasing level of cyber-separation.

Be logical, not emotional

Before you start thinking about the rules for acceptable use within your home, ask yourself the following question: 'What concerns you the most when your child uses digital technology at home?' Some self-awareness

> *I wish my mum would talk to me more. She's always on her phone texting friends, even when we have dinner.*
> **Six-year-old girl, Auckland**

is essential here. You need to understand what is driving your reactions, and whether they are emotional and reactive, or whether they are logical and well-thought through.

Your child has a right to use digital technology, and so the rules within the home need to be fair and meet the needs of each child, based on age and level of maturity. Spending time online researching a school project is in harmony with the child's educational commitments. Playing Minecraft or replying to text messages may not be educational, but they are important ways for your child to relax and build social networks. It is all just a matter of balance.

It is also important not to be bound by your own definition of how to efficiently achieve work-related goals. In the twentieth century, work typically had a daily time span of eight hours, and after that we had time to recharge, relax and do things we enjoyed. As well, the transition from work to play was instant and easily observed.

This is not the case today. If you walk into the house and observe your teenager writing up her conclusion on the history of human rights for a school assignment, but also responding to a text message from her friend telling her that netball has been cancelled due to poor weather, and then tweeting out to the world about how important it is that human rights should be taught in school, you are seeing a very different, modern phenomena. If you applied the old eight-hour frame of reference, it could be argued that your child is not focused – a test that always fails when applied to the contemporary child.

Today's teenagers interact on multiple levels, some observable and some not. A girl sitting on a couch completing an assignment, talking to a friend and informing the world about something she has learned is goal-orientated, sharing ideas, contributing positively to society and

> *Development is about opportunities, so parents have a duty to give kids opportunities in all the domains we expect them to develop skills. From looking at faces and smiling, to hearing language, to using language, to climbing, jumping, kicking and catching, to reading, writing, to computer games and skills.*
>
> *The problem comes when they have an unbalanced set of opportunities and develop some at the expense of others. There has always been specialisation of exposure to experiences, e.g. learning the violin in place of kicking a football. However, today this can be taken to extremes, with the lack of opportunities in talking face-to-face or group work in favour of screen time. Screens and digital communication are brilliant for some things. It is a matter of balance and opportunity.*
>
> **Nick Baker,**
> **Paediatrician, DHB Nelson**

communicating with a friend. I doubt that any parent would want to stop that.

When they are using DCT within the home, consider what it is they are doing on the computer. If it is constructive – a school-related activity, communicating with friends, being creative, reading an e-book – then we should be very careful not to condemn this. We also need to be aware of what we are modelling with our own personal use of digital technology.

There is a series of questions I like to ask teenage students concerning whether or not the adults in their lives are modelling an acceptable use of devices. The questionnaire asks them to respond to scenarios such as:

- While sitting down to have a family meal, do the adults in your household ever use computers, mobile phones, tablets or watch television at the table?

- Have you ever seen the adults in your household use their computer, mobile phone, tablet or watch television in their bedroom?

- Have you ever seen an adult sending or receiving a text message while driving a car? This includes waiting at traffic lights.

- Do you have pictures on the internet, perhaps on Facebook, that an adult family member has taken of you that you wished weren't on there?

- Do you think adults in your family should ask you for permission before they take a picture of you?

Every time I've given out this questionnaire, the responses from teenagers in schools has well over 65 per cent answering 'often' or 'sometimes' to all of these questions.

Our children learn from what we do, not from what we tell them. What we model today will either come back to embrace us or to bite us.

I really like it when my dad drives me to school, he talks to me lots because he can't use his phone.
Nine-year-old boy, Nelson

STRATEGIES FOR PARENTS

Acceptable use of screens within the home

- Children between birth and two years of age should not watch any TV or be exposed to any form of digital communication technology.

- For children between three and five years of age, the maximum time in front of a screen should not exceed one hour per day. You should confirm that the content you are exposing your children to is age-appropriate, and spend time co-viewing. Co-viewing reduces cyber-separation and allows the parent to emphasise key points, particularly when the game or theme in the programme or application is educational.[1]

- Consider using parental software applications to back-up your monitoring and to ensure the content is age-appropriate. Remember that these applications are to support you, not replace you as the parent.

- For younger children, consider the number of games they have on their device. For example, let them choose three and if they want another application, they need to delete one of the three.

- For younger members of the family, don't allow digital devices in the bedroom. Have them in a family space where you can keep an eye on them. This will also support healthy sleep patterns.

- Ensure that your older children do not expose younger siblings to online games or content that is inappropriate for their age.

- Try not to use a computer/device as a form of babysitting for a young child. Historically televisions played this role, and although too much TV also has its problems, computers are not the same as a TV. Often a busy parent/caregiver who uses the computer to keep a child entertained does not have time to properly monitor what the child is doing or watching.

- From age 5 to 18, there are no hard and fast rules. You will have to develop consistent rules that ensure a balanced life, with activities away from the screen, and healthy family time. Remember that children and teenagers like and need boundaries. The world feels safer with boundaries and it means they know where they should and shouldn't be in it.

- Create rules around the evening meal, for example 30 minutes before dinner everyone in the family stops using their digital devices, and no one goes back on them until 30 minutes after dinner is finished. This is a very effective strategy for reducing cyber-separation and for building family relationships.

- In the mornings, encourage no digital devices to be used until all household chores are completed, including getting ready for school.

- Consider having a technology-free day or evening once a week, and/or choose an activity that you can all participate in. Families that play together stay together.

- From time to time play an online game with your child, and try to get the whole family involved. This will help build relationships and reduce the effects of cyber separation.

- When you are on a device and your child approaches for a chat or asks for help, stop using your device, make eye contact with them and listen to what they have to say. You must model the behaviour you expect from your children.

- When your child is using a device and you want to talk to them, teach them to stop using their device and look at you and listen.

- If your child gets *down and out* get them *out and about*. Sometimes it's just time to disconnect, especially if they get overwhelmed by hyper-connection: fast transitions, bright lights, incoming text messages, Facebook updates and much more. If you see them getting moody and discontented, get them outside to kick a ball or go for a walk.

- Teach your child to put the phone away when anyone comes to visit. Good old-fashioned manners will never lose their relevance, even in the digital age.

- If your child has created an account or uses an online service of any kind that you don't have enough knowledge of, do the following:

  Find out what the site is for: is it a social network, can you share images, how does it make money out of your child's use?

Find out what information your child has provided during registration: have they given their email address, name, physical address, used a credit card, etc?

Identify the types of safety measures/controls the site has to offer you or the child: can you make it private, or is all content uploaded publicly accessible; can you report to someone if your child is harassed or threatened?

Identify the types of functionality the site has, especially communication functionality: does it have video streaming, a chatroom embedded into the site or game, for example?

If you are not comfortable with the application or service, delete it and explain to your child why you have done so.

PART 2

CHAPTER 7

ONLINE SEXUAL PREDATORS

Giving your child the control, not the stranger

The threat of online sexual predators is by far the biggest concern of parents when I talk to them about keeping their children safe online, and this is understandable. As parents we are wired to protect our young from danger and keep them safe. That's our job. Who would have imagined 15 years ago that today's parents have to live with the threat of a stranger in any location on the planet communicating with their child, at any time of the day or night.

An online sexual predator is a person who uses digital communication technology and internet-related services to locate, target and groom children and young people for the purpose of sexually abusing them. This can include abusing them in the physical world, or using other forms of online abuse, such as manipulating a child into performing sexually explicit acts online. Parents tell me that one of their major concerns is that they can't be with their child at all times, to see who they are talking to online or what they are talking about. However, parents do have a number of ways of supporting their child when they can't be with them, especially when the child is young.

Software applications are excellent tools that give parents control over their child's use of technology. The applications offer parents a range of options including control over the amount of time a child spends on a device and the type of content they are accessing on the internet.

It is important to remember that these applications are more suited when the child is young, rather than when they move out of adolescence and need to start asserting their independence. Friends become as important as family, and these friendships take on a deeper meaning. This is also the time when young people start to become aware of their own sexuality.

This period is a significant time in a child's online world. Risks increase because they are starting to explore their place in the world, as well as it being so easy to meet other people in a digital world. Parental controls at this age *can* support your risk management but they should not replace real, hands-on parenting.

As a child moves into this stage of their personal development they need to be supported by loving, compassionate and non-judgemental parents and caregivers, who continue to wrap them in their family values, and provide the child with knowledge about the world in which they live, to help them protect themselves.

We can't always be with our children, and in my opinion, it isn't healthy to even try. If we stifle children with constant attempts to be present in their lives and don't let them go, we will weaken their ability to protect themselves when they are on their own. Of course, these years of our child's life still require parental support and guidance, but it needs to be measured against their own developmental needs.

Sexual grooming

Sexual grooming refers to actions, both offline and online, deliberately undertaken with the aim of befriending and establishing an emotional connection with a child, in order to lower the child's natural defences in preparation for sexual abuse. It is a criminal offence.

Though this chapter is more about online sexual grooming, it is worth being reminded how paedophiles operate in the physical offline world. They often deliberately build a profile of themselves, which results in those around the child, including the wider community, seeing them as an upstanding and trustworthy person, such as them contributing to the welfare of a community by offering their time, skills or knowledge. They may have ascended to a position of authority or gained a position of trust, and this respected position provides the paedophile with immediate trust within the community. However, it should also be remembered that many sexual abusers are already known to the family and child.

Online grooming

'Online grooming is the act of sending an electronic message with indecent content to a recipient whom the sender believes to be under

16 years of age, with the intention of procuring the recipient to engage in or submit to sexual activity with another person, including, but not necessarily, the sender.'[2]

It is often easier and faster for predators to groom children online than in the offline world. **Paedophiles understand that at certain times of the day the number of children who are online increases and that children tend to accept and trust people more easily when they meet online rather than in the physical world**.

There are numerous opportunities predators will take to try to initiate contact with a child online. These include, but are not limited to, the places children go to online with their social media platforms, online gaming platforms, establishing connections via downloaded applications and smart phones.

In these online locations predators will 'surveil' and target potential victims, attempting to learn about what the child likes to do, what their interests are, what they may be struggling with at school or at home. All of this can be often found within the child's social media platforms, by watching the child exchange posts with friends or when playing online games. **The predator will use what they have learned about the child to build a relationship, perhaps by initiating conversations about a particular sport, interest or problem the child is struggling with**. The child starts to believe they share a common interest, and a bond develops between the predator and the child.

The predator may leverage this information found in the child's online social network, for example, if a girl has an argument with her father, and in a moment of poor judgement posts a comment online saying how much she hates him, this can be exploited. The predator could use this negative comment to drive a wedge between the girl and her father, the goal being to separate the child from parental care and oversight, and it also creates cyber-separation.

The online world is a **target-rich, offender-friendly environment**. It provides predators with a level of security and anonymity not available to them when they attempt to groom children in the physical space. As well as parental oversight being usually not as vigilant, predators can target larger numbers of children from one location, in relative safety, while using distance to protect themselves. This distance obviously places a child at a disadvantage because he or she cannot see the person in front of them.

Real world versus online world

One of the most dangerous myths that is perpetrated in the area of cyber-safety is that the offline, or physical, world is somehow more real that the online world. This has dangerous implications. Not only does it encourage the idea that the offline world is more significant, with more risks than the online world, but it also disempowers parents. **Parents need to realise that the guidelines and values of the physical world are just as transferable and essential in their child's online world.**

Parents want their child to conduct themselves safely and appropriately online in the same way they expect them to act in the physical world. Parents will say, 'You shouldn't connect to strangers online, you don't know them and you wouldn't do that in the real world.' And there is the problem right there: the child is being brought up thinking that one world is real and the other is not. If we want children to act in the same appropriate manner in both environments we must stop labelling one as real and one as not. To a 12-year-old gamer, the online world is very real, as real as the golf course his parent might walk around every Sunday morning.

One simple way we can break down this idea of a divide between offline and online worlds is to use words, especially with young children, which support the concept that when online, a child is going to a location. **If a child grows up experiencing the online world as a place they go *to*, rather than one that comes to them, they are more likely to use the knowledge and skills their parents have modelled in the offline world when they go online.**

When I talk with teenagers about how a paedophile uses surveillance and target selection to groom a child online, I give the following example. The example describes the internet as a location a person goes to and exists within.

Brianna goes to Facebook, she is 15 and has been going there since she was 12; it's her favourite hangout, she goes there after school most days. She has over 900 Facebook friends. Some of her friends don't talk to her, in fact, Brianna has forgotten they're there. One day while hanging out in Facebook after school, a friend request comes in from someone she doesn't know. His picture looks nice so she lets him into her Facebook hangout. She has so many friends in Facebook she can't talk with everybody, and anyway, most just seem to hang around the edges watching her and her friends from school talk and share pictures. Brianna is fine with this, and from time to time she does hear from some of these people.

One day while talking with one of her school friends, her new friend suggests they go somewhere else. He says, 'I hear that the town called Instagram is the place to hang out these days.' This new friend has really helped her recently. Brianna wants to go to Camp America but her dad has said no, because they can't afford it. In a moment of frustration, she'd vented in Facebook, saying, 'I hate my dad because he won't let me go to Camp America'. Her new friend has helped her through this, meeting her in Facebook every day and talking about her problems.

So they leave Facebook and travel the internet highway separately, arriving at Instagram town. Because both entered and registered to come and go as they please, now they have their own place in Instagram town. Back in Facebook, they'd given each other their Instagram addresses so they could find each other easily and visit.

Another friend in Facebook, one who hangs around on the periphery of Brianna's Facebook but doesn't talk to her, makes a note of the place that Brianna is going to in Instagram and he makes a note of her address also; he thinks he should pay her a visit. He decides to follow Brianna there.

This follower is a paedophile who has been watching Brianna for over two years now, from the edges of her Facebook hangout. He knows her likes, her dislikes, he knows where her mum and dad work and he knows she doesn't like her dad at the moment. He arrives at Instagram and looks her up, using her address. He knocks on her door in her hangout, and waits. She accepts his request and lets him in. He starts to send her pictures of America and of young people going on Camp America trips.

She really likes the pictures and still dreams that one day she will go, too. She puts a picture up in her Instagram hangout and he comments on it and tells her it's amazing. He then invites her to his place in Instagram. Brianna leaves her place and goes to meet him. When she arrives at his place she sees so many pictures of America and camping. And even pictures of Labradors – her favourite dog; in fact, she happens to have a Labrador.

She has a closer look at this stranger and what he does and from what she can tell, he arranges for people to come to America to go camping. Brianna plucks up the courage and asks him if he'll help her get to Camp America. He says, 'Of course I will. Let's go and hang out at a great place I know called SKYPE town ... click on this link and follow me. Brianna is so excited. She follows him.

If we start talking to children, especially young ones, about the internet as being a location, it has the potential to do two things. It allows the child to take the skills that Mum and Dad have given to keep them safe offline, such as in a park, online, and it allows Mum and Dad to use the same parental enquiry they do offline, online.

Talking to strangers

A common refrain that parents use with their children to protect them from online predators is 'Don't talk to strangers'. Unfortunately, this piece of advice is completely unrealistic because if they can't talk to strangers online, then they may as well throw their technology away. What we need to be saying is, 'We are going to teach you how to talk to strangers, when the need arises.'

Any child that blogs to the world is already communicating with strangers; any child that uploads videos of themselves to YouTube is communicating with strangers; any child that plays an online game with players they have never met in the physical space is already talking to strangers.

The reality of our children's online world is that it is full of strangers, so asking them not to talk to strangers is setting them up to fail. And we'd have also failed to use the opportunity to empower them.

The skill we need to develop in a child is how to leave out personal information when talking to strangers online. Fortunately, this skill has been taught to children long before their digital world developed. Think about when a child goes to the shops with an adult and how many strangers the adult encounters. This could be exchanging pleasantries with a supermarket checkout operator, providing directions to a stranger who is lost, asking for assistance at the local library – an adult will interact with many people. The child watches this interaction over the years and learns that how you talk to people who are not part of your family or social group is different to how you talk to people you know. They acquire this skill through parental modelling, and it is a skill that is transferable to the online world.

Linking

I've delivered presentations to thousands of parents all across New Zealand and I can always reliably prove to them that they *do* have the knowledge and skills to keep their child safe from predators online.

I use a technique called linking, which shows the similarity between the physical and online worlds, and how a divide does not need to exist between them.

Here is how linking works: In scenario 1, the 10-year-old boy is at the park, his mum has knowledge of the place, including how far it is away from home, a general idea of who usually goes there and that the park is suitable for children. The child may even meet new children there. When the boy comes home, his mum will often ask questions about whether he enjoyed himself and who he talked to and played with.

In scenario 2, the boy is in an online game chatting to his friends and other players in the game, some of whom he has never met in the physical space. His mum knows the child is in a suitable game, the game is age appropriate, and she knows where he is at home.

Both scenarios have much in common, except for how the mum relates to them.

In scenario 1 she asks her son, 'Did you enjoy yourself and who did you talk to?' But in scenario 2, she doesn't ask this. Most parents never ask the same type of questions when their child finishes playing an online game as opposed to playing in the physical world. There are a number of reasons for this but I would suggest that, in part, society hasn't found the language yet to ask those questions.

When a teenager comes home from a party at 1 a.m., a parent or caregiver will inevitably want to know about it: 'How did you get on; who did you meet?' But if that same teenager comes out of the bedroom after spending three hours in a town called Instagram, there isn't language yet that a parent/caregiver can access to enquire about that three-hour gap. The town called Instagram isn't regarded as a place, seeing it only exists in a two-dimensional space. Only by imagining this

LINKING

Comparing the offline world to the online world

Safeguarding children in the offline world	Safeguarding children in the online world
Scenario 1 Going to the park	**Scenario 2** Playing online
Safeguarding rules	**Safeguarding rules**
1) You can go for 1 hour then come home. 2) Don't talk to any strangers. If anyone tries to talk to you, walk away, come home and tell me. 3) If anybody bothers you or worries you walk away, come home and tell me. 4) Play nicely with other boys and girls. 5) Don't go off anywhere else.	1) You can play for 1 hour then turn it off. 2) Don't talk to any strangers about personal things. 3) If anybody tries to talk to you about personal things that are unrelated to the game, stop communicating, leave the computer and come and tell me. 4) Play nicely with other boys and girls. 5) Don't go off anywhere else.
Mum decides to go to the park to make sure her child is OK and see who he is playing with.	Mum decides to sit down with her child to make sure he's OK and to see who he's playing with.

space as three-dimensional will we start to access and use the language we have already acquired.

When your child goes online, they are leaving home and going to another location. The online world is an extension of the physical space your child lives in. It is no less real. **Our job is to provide our child with the knowledge, guidance and rules to stay safe from strangers, just as we would when our child is at the park down the road.**

An alternative scenario 1: Going to the park

Let's say this time an adult stranger approaches the child in the park and tries to persuade him to leave and go to another location. The child knows not to talk to this person; he knows to walk away and go home and tell an adult or somebody else he trusts. He also knows if necessary to kick and scream and make lots of noise, but under no circumstances should he go with the stranger. And if this boy walks off and alerts his friends to this dangerous situation, the boy has relied on the modelling and guidance his parents have given him. **The boy is in control, not the stranger**.

An alternative scenario 2: Playing on his computer

In this scenario, the boy is playing with others online, when another player he has never met asks him for a picture of himself. The boy doesn't like this question as it is personal and has nothing to do with the game they're playing. He ignores it and carries on playing. Later, during the same session, the 'stranger' player asks him what school he goes to, and how old he is. He replies, 'I can't talk about that, sorry.' The player then asks him to click on a link. By this time the boy has had enough, he stops communicating, and he tells an adult. He remembers his parents' advice, that somebody asking you to follow them online to another location is the same as a stranger in the park asking you to go somewhere else with them. **The boy is in control, not the stranger**. An example like this illustrates the strong link between the offline and online worlds, and that the same strategies can be taught and used by your child to keep them safe in both places.

The architecture of the online world can seem complicated and daunting. But there are simple strategies you can use to keep your child safe, using the knowledge and skills you already have. Remember, firstly, that if your child comes to you and reports that a stranger has been asking them inappropriate questions, give them a big hug and tell them how proud you are of them for coming and telling you.

One of the most important pathways to supporting and keeping your child safe is to give them the confidence to be able to come and talk to you about *anything*. Developing open lines of communication with your child is a major step towards ensuring their online safety, and it is essential that you keep your 'tiger' under control.

When a parent approaches me for support or discloses something to me that I believe needs to be reported to the police, they will often hesitate, indicating they can't bring themselves to enter a police station and talk about the problem in an open forum. 'What if somebody else is in the reception area?' they'll often ask. If you need to go to your local police to discuss any matter of safety, it is vital you know you can, and that you can be received in a way that supports your intention. This is backed up by the following message from Senior Constable John O'Donovan (New Zealand Police, retired):

> *Taking a young person into a police station to make a report or to seek help can be an uncomfortable, anxious time. It is important to know that a member of the public is allowed to say to the person at the front desk that what they have to discuss is a sensitive matter and that they would like to see an officer in a private interview room. Do not say anything that may embarrass you or the young person where other members of the public can hear. This is vital in setting the scene for making even a serious matter more positive.*

What you can do if you believe your child is being groomed online

- Contact the police without delay.

- Remove the opportunity for the grooming to continue. In the short-term this may include removing the devices being used.

- Don't panic, and choose your words carefully when you talk to your child. How you talk will set the tone for how you and your family move through this event and out the other side. Make sure you communicate how much you love them, and that this is not their fault.

- If possible capture any evidence of the grooming. This could include messages sent and/or received on the devices used. Take screen shots of the web pages, record the web addresses, save emails and secure any text messages sent or received. It is important to preserve as much evidence as possible.

- Even if you do not believe you have evidence, you should still contact the police as there may be other methods available to gather evidence. Your child's devices may be required by the police to do this.

- If you feel that your child is not coping well – perhaps they won't leave their bedroom, they've stopped talking to you or don't want to leave the house – consider offering your child the opportunity to talk to a therapist, perhaps arranged via your doctor.

- As the parent/caregiver, make sure you look after yourself at the same time. Don't be afraid to ask for help, and consider going to see your doctor or asking a trusted friend to support you. The important thing is to talk to someone about how you're feeling.

- It is imperative you keep your cyber-tooth tiger under control, and not let your anxieties become your child's anxieties. They need to form a healthy relationship with this technology, as it will inevitably be a major part of their life.

- Once you have moved through the event and life gets back to normal, stay connected to your child's online world; do not let cyber-separation form. It is important to keep an eye on them to see how they are coping. Are they social, do they have friends, are they open and goal-orientated and back to the child you know and love? Keep the lines of communication open and remember to make sure that they know how much you love them.

- If you are not connected to your child via their social networks, consider asking them if you can join, reminding your child you are not there to judge or police them, but to offer guidance should the need arise. As well, ask to have access to their mobile phones so that you can also offer support.

- Finally, go out and treat you and your child to something special – you will have deserved it.

Online sexual grooming is a scary and very real part of the online world. A couple of real-life situations with families and how we have dealt with these situations follows:

'Send me a naked picture'

I was asked to work with Ariana, a 14-year-old girl who had formed an online relationship with a male who she thought was 19 and living in the USA. Ariana had sent naked pictures of herself to him, at his request. At the time, she did not see herself as a victim or that she was in danger. Her parents, however, had noticed a change in her behaviour. She'd become very protective of both her phone and computer, and she refused to let anyone have access to it. She was also spending far more time on her computer, especially late at night, and always in her bedroom. She'd become secretive and agitated when they tried to talk to her about their concerns.

When an opportunity presented itself, they had a look at the text messages on her phone and were horrified to find she had sent multiple sexualised text messages, as well as images of herself, partially clad, to somebody called Mike. When confronted, she was unwilling to stop communicating with him and would use any means possible to connect with him, through wi-fi at school or any accessible network she could connect to outside of the home. Her parents' response was to take away all forms of technology from her, which is the point where I became involved.

During my first session with Ariana, I explained that I was not there to judge her, deceive her or try to make her tell me anything she didn't want to talk about in relation to the person she had met online.

I wanted her to know that her family were concerned for her safety and well-being. I made it clear that my hope was she'd stop sending the pictures and stop communicating with Mike, because he almost certainly didn't have her best interests at heart.

When working with a minor who is the potential victim of online sexual predation, I require two things to happen. Firstly, I or the guardian inform the police of the girl's situation. Secondly, I will suggest a psychologist meet with the child. In these situations, safeguarding children offline or online usually requires a multi-agency approach; the necessary organisations collaborate and share knowledge, skills and experience. (It is worth noting here that often a psychologist or police is not required.)

My next step with Ariana was to find out from her how the online relationship had begun, what form it had taken, and what she thought the future was.

Ariana believed Mike's claim that he was 19. She'd met him via social media after accepting a friend request from him. Over the following weeks they'd communicated through social media and text messaging. Eventually this included Skype sessions. He'd also started communicating with her friends via social media. Ariana believed that Mike planned to come to New Zealand to work, when they would be able to travel together throughout New Zealand.

One of my goals during these early sessions is to demonstrate how online predators use various tactics to manipulate victims, using attention, affection and in many cases gifts as a means of building a bond between predator and victim. The hope is that the person involved begins to see similarities between my examples and his/her own situation. Around this stage, I also introduce the victim to the idea of their own digital boundary and how it can help to protect them, and what cyber-muscles are.

We discuss what enables predators, when they're selecting potential targets for online grooming. Young children and teenagers often talk online about personal things in their lives, including likes, dislikes, interests, hopes and intentions; access to this information supports a paedophile's objective.

We then move on to target-hardening and discuss the protective strategies that can be used. This involves teaching how to talk to strangers online, the types of pictures it is OK to post, online friends, and learning how to use the security functionality within the platform.

Scene-setting teaches a victim how to handle stressful situations online, where a situation is created and they tell you how they themselves would react. I discuss 'repelling', which teaches how to react at the first point of contact with a person they feel uncomfortable with, and 'reporting', teaching them to connect with a person they trust, identifying the different agencies and support groups that she/he or their friends can contact for help, and also using their parents, guardians or their Lighthouse.

After the third session with Ariana, she had started to trust me and talk about some of the conversations she was having with Mike. She told him she could not send any more pictures of herself to him, which, according to Ariana, upset him. He had also started spending a lot more time talking to Ariana's friends through Facebook. Ariana could see some of these exchanges. The situation had become even worse for Ariana because Mike was throwing a party online and had invited her friends to it. I asked her how she felt and she said she felt angry, guilty, sad, jealous and sorry that she'd told Mike she couldn't send pictures.

Because Ariana was struggling with this decision and feeling so many emotions, I decided to lay my cards on the table and told her I believed Mike was a predator. He was certainly showing all the characteristics of one: he was 19, she was 14; he had made her feel sad, jealous and angry; he was using his supposed friendships with her friends as leverage to make her feel guilty, in the hope that she eventually would send more pictures of herself to him.

I reminded her of our discussion as to why predators want images. This can include selling them to other predators, using them in paedophile magazines or for self-gratification. I also informed her that what Mike was doing was illegal. I asked Ariana to think about her digital boundary and tell me if she was inside it or outside of it at present. She said she was inside it. When I asked why, she said, 'Because I won't send him pictures any more'. I agreed, pointing out she was flexing her cyber-muscles. Ariana was powering up.

'What should I do?' she asked. I said she needed to stop the communication, get her friends to do the same and that we could assist with this by talking to their parents. She became very emotional and decided that it *was* time to stop talking to him. She was upset when she realised he wasn't coming to New Zealand to take her touring. He didn't actually love her and it was all just a big lie. She told me she felt stupid and ashamed. I said, 'I have worked with 22-year-olds who have been deceived in the same way you've been deceived. I've worked with senior citizens who have given thousands of dollars to cyber-criminals over the internet. It can happen to anyone.' I told her she was brave and very much loved by her family.

Remember, a victim is a victim whether it's in the physical space or the online world; one is not more real than the other. Even when a child or teenager does not identify as a victim or does not believe the person is a paedophile, when they feel that the relationship is built on respect, trust and love – even if that child or teenager has been sexually abused and they actually want the relationship to continue, they are still the victim. It is so important not to judge, not to overreact and to keep the lines of communication open.

'Let's meet up'

One evening I was heading home and my phone rang. It was a woman who sounded frantic and on the verge of tears. She told me her name was Sandra and that a friend had recommended she call me. She said she'd discovered her daughter, Maia, who was 13, had formed an online relationship some months earlier with a boy called Jackson, who she initially thought was 14. Sandra did not like the connection her daughter had made and tried her best to get her daughter to stop. Maia refused and cyber-separation had crept in between them. This reduced her mother's ability to support her child online and offline. Maia was starting to isolate herself.

That afternoon Sandra had discovered the boy online was actually 24. Looking at the text messages on her mobile phone, it appeared Jackson was arranging to meet Maia, as he lived in the same area. Some of the text messages clearly showed he had declared his real age because of the fact he was going to meet her. Maia at first had appeared uneasy and upset by his latest declaration, but eventually her unease had subsided, and talk continued about meeting him.

Maia has begun trading on two things: 1) she has developed feelings for him; 2) she knows he lied. It is possible that if he had declared his real age at the start, she may have withdrawn. However, because she now has feelings for him she trades away the truth about his age. Maia is now outside of her digital boundary.

I asked where Maia was, and her mother told me she'd run out of the house in response to her challenging her on the text messages and his age. I took Sandra's name and contact details and told her to call the police and to give them as much information as she could about this man, including any screen shots from the online encounters. I asked her to immediately start looking for her daughter, and to contact Maia's friends and her friends' parents.

The next day Sandra called to say she'd found her daughter sitting down the road from their house and she'd asked her to come home. She'd called the police and passed on all the information about Jackson. The mother asked if I could meet with her daughter and talk about the dangers of the situation she had been through. The meeting with Maia was similar to the process I had worked through with Ariana. By the end Maia was remorseful and said she couldn't believe how stupid she'd been; that she felt terrible for the pain and worry she had caused her family.

She told me she'd met him through Facebook and they seemed to like all the same things, and how it had been 'just brilliant' that she had someone who really understood her. They liked the same music, fashion and food. I asked her to think about how many times she had posted personal information about her likes and dislikes, about arguments she may have been having with her parents, online, and she looked at me and said, 'How could I be so stupid? My whole life is on Facebook. I'm going to delete my account.'

I explained that she didn't need to; that she had a right to use technology, and she could be just as safe online as in the physical space, so long as she took control of technology and not let it control her.

'At last things are looking up'

Steve goes to Facebook one evening and accepts a friend request from a girl he has never met in the physical space. She seems nice and is good looking. Over the next few weeks they regularly meet on Facebook and post messages to each other. The girl, Bella, says she's unable to Skype due to limited wi-fi access, and apparently her father doesn't allow her to have a mobile phone.

Steve looks forward every day to exchanging messages with Bella. Over the past few months he has been feeling very low – lots of school work to keep up with, his part-time job is getting him down, he has no idea of what he wants to do when he leaves school and three weeks ago he broke up with his girlfriend.

His friends on Facebook had also noted he was becoming quite dark, talking about how 'stuffed up' life is and that the break-up with his girlfriend was just another example of how horrible life is right now. Bella has turned everything around for him, he's excited about life and his parents are so pleased for him and relieved his attitude is more positive.

One morning Steve gets up and sees an unopened message on his phone. It's from Bella, telling him she's finally got a phone but not sure how long she's going to have it. Another message, and this time it's a picture of her, lying naked on a bed. Another message comes through: 'I hope you like it'. Then a message saying, 'I can't wait for us to meet up. Please send me a picture of you like mine'.

That evening Steve takes a naked picture of himself and sends it to her. He can't believe how his luck has changed and how happy he feels. He can't stop thinking about when they will meet up and what it will be like. But when he gets up the next morning he has another message on his phone from her: 'Send me more naked pics now. If you don't, I'm going to put the one I've got up on Facebook for all your mates to see.'

I became aware of this incident when Steve's parents approached me after a workshop I had just delivered and told me what had happened to their boy. They wanted to know what to do. I asked them how they'd become aware of it and the father said his son had told them after two days of stressing and not sleeping. Steve's father said his son had not sent any more pictures.

His mother was also hurting and deeply worried for her son. What was reassuring for me in this situation was the way both parents expressed their love and concern for their child. They saw him as a victim and wanted to protect him and help him and, importantly, they were not judging him. It was very telling of the open, loving and trusting relationship Steve had with his parents.

Being able to tell a parent/caregiver everything is a major contributor to online safety and offline safety. Children and young people make mistakes. That is their right. They also have the right to protection, to be nurtured, and to an open line of communication back to parents/caregivers when they make mistakes.

Had Steve felt he couldn't talk about what had happened, he may have sent more pictures, trying to control the situation, and/or have spiralled towards depression.

I indicated I would work with their son, which may include contacting the police, securing any evidence, and also connecting him with other organisations that could support him.

Towards the end of the meeting I asked the mother how she was coping and she burst into tears, so worried for her son, so worried that the naked picture her son had sent would eventually find its way onto Facebook for his friends to see. It is often the case that parents are deeply impacted by the mistakes their child makes online. I recommended she make an appointment to see her doctor with the intention of seeing a therapist to support her and her husband if necessary.

STRATEGIES FOR PARENTS

How to prevent online grooming

- Explain to your child the similarities between the offline world and the online world. This will help your child use the skills they already have in the physical world to stay safe when online.

- Children and young people need to be taught how to communicate online. This means they need to establish a digital boundary first, and learn what *not* to talk about, including phone numbers, what school they go to, how old they are, other family information, such as names of brothers and sisters or where their parents work, and home addresses.

- Teach your young children never to send pictures of themselves or family members to friends online, unless the parent/caregiver gives permission.

- Teach them not to upload images of themselves sitting in their bedroom. This is a private location and it can draw predators in towards them.

- User names in online games should not be your child's real name. Teach them to create an internet name.

- Teach your child that what they broadcast should be consistent with your family values. Pictures and information your child uploads should not be flirty, risqué or sexual. This also includes any email address your child creates, or the messages they leave on their phones. Online predators will trawl the internet and become interested when they find this kind of content.

- Teach your child not to accept friend requests from people they don't know. Predators rely on and can exploit young people's trusting natures.

- Many children spend a lot of unsupervised time online every day. From time to time look at what your child is doing online and check the sites they visit.

- Parental monitoring software is available to install to support your role as a guardian.

- Reiterate to your child that when playing an online game or when broadcasting information in a public forum on the internet, they must leave out all personal information. Talking about personal things signals to a predator that they are vulnerable. They must present themselves as powerful and in control.

- Discuss with your child that they must not talk about personal problems online. If they need help or advice, encourage them to speak in person to you or a trusted friend. You could also show them the list of support agencies on pages 152–55. Children who are confused about their sexuality and who talk about their issues online can then be targeted by predators; children with issues such as low self-esteem, their weight or their appearance, and who then discuss these things online are exposing their vulnerabilities, which a predator will use to exploit a child.

- Teach your child never to accept a gift from a stranger offline or online. Predators have been known to send children phones so that they can communicate with them away from the security of parental oversight.

- If you see your child behaving secretively around their phone, or a phone you don't recognise, consider the possibility that they have been sent a phone by another party. This is often done in order to provide intimacy and to move grooming to the next level. Teenagers, in particular, will go to extraordinary lengths to protect their love interests.

- Teach your child never to accept requests from strangers who want to connect with them via web cams. Paedophiles and organised crime rings target young people and trick them into sending sexualised images or videos of themselves. This material is then used for self-gratification or on-sold to other paedophile rings. Sometimes young people are tricked into sending videos and images, and then are financially blackmailed and/or threatened to send more. This is sometimes referred to as 'sextortion'.

- Teach your child not to ignore their gut instincts. Encourage them that if the language being used seems inappropriate or sexualised,

STOP COMMUNICATION. And always reassure them that it is never too late to get out of a bad situation.

- For young people, it may be appropriate to use real-life situations from the news as a point of discussion, and to use as scene-setting to protect themselves in the present.

- Contact Netsafe if you need advice and help. See page 153 for details.

Important information

If you believe your child is in immediate danger because of threats via any form of information communication technology, contact the police by dialling 111. If you are unsure, still dial 111 and they will assist you. If the matter is not urgent, contact your local police station.

CHAPTER 8

SEXTING

Keeping it appropriate and knowing how to repel
unwanted attention

Sexting is when a person sends, receives or forwards sexual content in image, video or text message, using digital communication technology, including mobile phones and computers.

Having worked with so many children ranging in age from 9 to 18, and sometimes with both the child and their family, I have seen first-hand the devastating consequences of sexting. I should stress that some children are less affected by these events, bouncing back quickly, although most young people face a tremendous struggle to pick themselves back up when things go wrong and their intimate photos end up online.

Why do young people sext?

During my workshops with teenagers we often discuss why people might participate in sexting. The reasons put forward are numerous; some seem to reflect the ability of human beings to adapt to a changing world – people need to communicate and this new technology has simply provided another way to do this. Others point to underlying issues within the person sending or requesting the images. It appears to me, through these discussions, that there are underlying needs in all of us: we want to be seen, valued and heard. These are desires that, when not achieved, can mean some people will seek out novel ways of connecting with others to express themselves and be noticed.

Some students believe it is a modern form of flirting, giving an admirer the chance to let a potential partner know they like them without the added pressure of a face-to-face encounter. Others have suggested it allows partners to demonstrate how much they love and trust each other. Others see it as a form of currency, having to send the images to maintain a relationship. Some teenagers like to take risks that they believe will elevate their position within a group and when friends dare them to send images they feel compelled to comply. The influence of alcohol also contributes to this modern form of communication. Many teenagers suggest to me that sexting is becoming more acceptable.

However, it is one thing when a teenager asks a partner for images when there *isn't* an imbalance of power, meaning both parties are consenting. But if the person asking is in a position of control, for example, an ex who has already received images while they were a couple and now wants more, and are using the images as leverage: 'If you don't send more I will show other people the ones you have sent', and so on, then this is a very different, serious scenario. This is a form of manipulation; it is dangerous, destructive, and parents and teenagers should seek advice from the police.

'When they're scarred, they need love'

I met a mother who was desperate for help for her daughter, who had been severely bullied at school because of naked pictures she had sent to a boy, which found their way onto the internet.

I noted the mother was concerned with the poor choice her daughter had made, but her main worry was how she was reacting to the treatment from others within the community. She told me that her daughter wouldn't leave her bedroom, eat food or even look at her father. Her husband didn't know how to talk to his daughter about the issue.

We set up a plan for me to work with the girl, which would include scene-setting and target-hardening. However, I said that before we met, the best advice I could give her was the following: 'Go home, and both you and your husband go into her bedroom, jump on the bed on either side of her, wrap her in your arms, pull her in tight to both of you and tell her how much you love her. Surround her with your love.'

A few months later I saw the mother again. She approached me and gave me a hug. She was a very different person to the sad, anxious mother I had first seen. She said she'd followed my advice, and she and her husband did exactly what I had suggested. She said it was the first time she'd seen her husband cry, holding his daughter.

She said when they now sit down and talk about making better decisions in the future, her daughter has a smile on her face. When her father had asked, 'Why are you smiling? This is serious stuff,' his daughter replied, 'When I hated myself, when I was ashamed of myself, when I felt very alone, you told me you loved me and you would protect me. I will never forget that, Dad, and when I have children and they make mistakes I'm going to tell them what you told me. I love you so much.' And as you can imagine, he shed a few tears again.

When a child feels alone in the world and/or ashamed of themselves, when they are scarred, they need love. They have a right to make mistakes, and far more important than the poor choices they make is how we react to them once they become a victim. Compassion and empathy are powerful healers that can dramatically reduce the emotional healing time a victim needs to recover.

I made a mistake and sent a nude pic to a boy at school. Other students at the school were sent copies of the picture. One boy said if I didn't send him more pics he was gonna tell my dad. I felt sick and really scared. I stopped eating and would cry a lot at night. A girl who wasn't even my friend at school found out what was happening. She came up to me one day at school and told me that you'd said kids have the right to make mistakes and she said she would help me. She went with me to see the principal in the school, and then she helped me talk to my dad, who was really upset and I'd felt so alone that I couldn't tell him. I will never forget the look on the boy's face when the principal told the boy the police had been notified and wanted to talk to him. I will never forget the girl who stood up for me, she is so fantastic. My mum actually cried and hugged her for protecting me.

Fourteen-year-old girl, Hamilton

Impact on the wider family

A 13-year-old girl had sent several explicit pictures of herself to a boy she met online. The boy, who resided outside of New Zealand, threatened to post them online. We worked through the situation and fortunately for the girl and the family we managed to take control of the situation. Twelve months later I bumped into the mother. She indicated her daughter was happy and enjoying life, but she explained how much it had affected her personally. She eventually went to her GP who prescribed medication and therapy.

It is important to remember that often when parents or guardians become aware that their child is the victim of sexting, the home can become a hostile place. Everyone is affected, but the impact on other family members can sometimes be overlooked.

When working with families, I make a point of asking the parents/caregivers how they are feeling. And on many occasions they will describe the personal pain and sadness they feel, often compounded by a lack of control or the perceived belief that they cannot protect their child.

A father may feel that his child is not who he thought he/she was and it can cause him to say things to the child he will later regret – and his child will never forget. This reaction often amplifies the seriousness of the situation. A mother can often blame herself and the guilt she carries affects her ability to function. Siblings, especially younger ones, can be deeply affected by the impact on a sister or a brother, and of course are themselves victims because the home has become toxic and unpredictable.

If people within the wider community should start to talk about the family, then two environments in which the child lives and communicates have dramatically changed in a short space of time. Meanwhile, all of this is being witnessed and experienced by the child who sent the content, who could have become isolated from their social group at school and outside of it. Some in that group might start spreading rumours, talking negatively about the child online, pointing at them in the school hallway, waiting for them as they approach the school – not to support them but to harass or bully them. That one word 'sexting', like so many other labels in society, hides the pain and the impact on victims who are caught out by a moment's lack of judgement or peer pressure. And one of the hardest types of victim to deal with is the one who does not see themselves as a victim or their behaviour as risky.

The right to make a mistake

Too often I hear adults, including some cyber-safety experts, teachers and parents, claiming that once you post an image it's online forever and there is nothing you can do about it. There is actually a lot that can be done to help a young person who has a derogatory digital footprint. Telling someone otherwise is a dangerous message to spread.

I am very aware when working with groups of students that some may have uploaded pictures that they later regret, while there may also be victims of sexting within the audience I'm speaking to. I am also asked to visit schools where a sexting incident has occurred.

Technically, it's true that an image, once posted to the internet, has the possibility of being there permanently. However, parents and/or the child can take action by contacting organisations such as Netsafe, who may be able to assist families and teenagers to have these images taken down. Their details can be found on page 153.

Also, it is a good idea to think of the internet as a pipe that is 50,000 kilometres deep and only 10 centimetres wide. We can view the width and the top 30 centimetres (pages 1–5 in a Google search) at any one time, but we can't view the entire length. So, consider a teenager who has a few images of himself drunk at a party. When a prospective

When you as a parent decide the police should be involved in any incident where your child has made a mistake or been compromised, your young person will often be so embarrassed by their actions, they will not disclose the full extent of what has occurred because of perceived disappointment to you. Your job is not to know the whole story but to encourage him/her to speak honestly and fully to the police officer taking the statement. Only then can the appropriate and/or legal response be given.

**Senior Constable John O'Donovan QSM,
New Zealand Police (Retired)**

employer does a Google search, the images appear; they're in the top 30 centimetres of the pipe (pages 1 & 2 of Google). But as a teenager creates content going forward, they will populate this pipe with other online content. This helps to push negative content down the pipe into the depth of its kilometres – or past page 5 of a Google search. It's true that if an employer wants to delve further they may find the content, but this is still a good approach to take, because even competing content that isn't negative is an advantage to have online, to at least show who the young person really is. Teenagers populate the internet almost daily so as long as they are mindful of what they post, it happens automatically; time is also a healer in cyberspace.

Saying 'it's there forever', or asking 'what will employers think about your child?' doesn't help in relation to a sexting issue, but it does amplify the pain the child and parents feel if the child is a victim of sexting.

When parents ask me for help, one of the first comments they make is: 'I don't know what to say to my child.' But this is one of the easiest problems to fix. Tell them you love them and hold them close.

Olivia and Liam

Olivia and Liam are both 14 years old and have been in a relationship for about three months; there is no imbalance of power. Both of them have been sending naked pictures of themselves to each other and both are outside of their digital boundaries.

The personal pictures found their way into the public domain after a boy at school uploaded them as a prank for others to see. The impact on Olivia and Liam was immediate. Rumours started spreading, some students posted nasty comments about them, adults who had no relationship to the situation other than to be living in the same small town were gossiping, and some were even telling their own children to stay away from Olivia and Liam.

During a session with Olivia she told me that nobody at school would talk to her except for two close friends who would meet her at the school gate and support her through the day. Olivia described the daily trauma of entering the classroom to have boys calling her derogatory names, laughing at her, and one boy taunting her that he had the images on his own mobile phone. And then she'd endure the same kind of treatment on the way home on the bus.

It is vital that people like Olivia and Liam can talk to parents or their Lighthouse, and have knowledge of the services available to help and support them should they find themselves in these extremely stressful situations.

To help Olivia, we set up regular contact with her school guidance counsellor, and I recommended that she visit her GP for possible referral to see a psychologist. Olivia was anxious, she felt lonely and she deeply regretted what she had done. She could see no way past the situation, had lost influence and control within her own social circle, and felt that she had completely lost her power.

Because Olivia needed help to deal with this hostile situation and to protect herself going forward, I did some scene-setting, which includes picking a situation that worries her and then asking her to show me how she would deal with it in the future. Scene-setting creates a safe environment for her to practise what to do if she finds herself in a situation that worries her, and it gives me the opportunity to tailor my advice to her specific needs.

I reinforced to Olivia that while it was incredibly embarrassing and hurtful to be treated like this, she could get past it and start to take back control and project her own power.

I asked her to imagine she could go back in time and was again walking into her classroom to have the boy taunt her, saying he had a picture of her on his mobile phone. This time I asked her to make a mental note of the time, the room she was in, what the boy said, who else witnessed what the boy said, and to then leave the room and record it all on her phone or notebook. It was important that she did not engage with the boy.

She then should take this information to the guidance counsellor and inform them she required the principal to be made aware of the situation and give them a copy of the notes. If the boy had downloaded or stored the image of her on his phone, she had the option of also telling the police. At the very least, however, by informing the school authorities and by keeping accurate notes, Olivia would be starting to defend herself, and letting others know that she was doing this – she would be starting to power up.

Projecting confidence and control in these situations helps protect Olivia from those who might also feel tempted to abuse her human rights and it target-hardens her.

In this particular incident, Liam also suffered from the mistreatment of others but he worked through the issue more quickly and from information I received was not impacted in the same way as his girlfriend. It would be a mistake to think that this is always the way. In my experience, the way society has dealt with males as victims has made it harder for them in this digital age to come forward and receive support.

Jack

I was approached by a mother and father who wanted advice on how to help Jack, their 16-year-old son, who had sent naked pictures to his girlfriend. The girl lost her phone and the person who found it uploaded the images of Jack for hundreds of people to see within his community. Jack was devastated, would not leave his room or go back to school and his mother had found him sobbing in his bedroom two days earlier.

My immediate concern is always whether the victim is safe, physically, and what is the state of their well-being. When I asked Jack's father about his son, his response was: 'He's fine, he just needs to toughen up. He sent them, it's his fault. He's an idiot and I'm disgusted with him.' The mother looked at me and said, 'He is not ok, he is hurt. My boy is hurt and I don't know what to do'.

It is obviously important that both parents be on the same page when it comes to supporting a child who is in harm's way. I advised them to take him to his GP for an assessment and possible referral to see a psychologist to help him. We would also work on how to get the images taken down and deal with any mistreatment by other people.

It emerged that over the past two years Jack had not had a good time at school. He had been bullied and could not seem to solidify any long-term friendships until he met this girl. But again, the father just said, 'He needs to toughen up.'

Jack's father's take on the situation and perhaps how he was raised himself is affecting his view of the bigger picture here. The father sees none of Jack's issues and is only choosing to focus on one poor choice.

I doubt very much that Jack would make the same mistake again or that he will forget this. I doubt, too, that he will forget the loneliness he felt – some of which can be attributed to his father. When I am dealing with situations like this, I always remind the young person that there are organisations where they can get the support they deserve if it is not available within the home.

Talk to your child about sexting and how they can prevent it

Open, non-judgemental communication with your child is the best way to help them stay safe when they go online. Talking about the dangers of sexting can be a difficult conversation for your child to willingly participate in, but it is essential. When you start this conversation, tell them how much you love them, talk about how proud you are of them and how valuable they are.

Your child's level of maturity, age and family values will determine what you talk about with your child. For the following, let's assume we are talking to parents with teenagers, however, you may feel that the following is applicable to your younger children also.

- Let them know you or their Lighthouse is always available to talk about sexting, on their terms. Remember, the role of the Lighthouse is to listen without judgement and link the child to the guardians. They are not required to know about sexting.

- Explain to them that regardless of who the person is in their life asking for the pictures/inappropriate content, they do *not* have their best interests at heart. If they find themselves being pressured to send pictures, ask them to stop and consider the motivation of the person asking. Often in these situations an imbalance of power is being established and sending material will leave them outside of their digital boundary.

- Talk to your child about what it means to deflect and repel: encourage them to find responses that take the 'heat' off themselves. If someone is pressuring them to send an inappropriate image, they can use lines such as 'Are you serious? My dad would blow a fuse and chase you out of town' to deflect the pressure.

- Remind them that relationships end and feelings for partners change. Sending pictures inside the relationship can feel safe, but often after the relationship ends, young people are left in an extremely vulnerable situation, having now lost control of their intimate photos.

- Point out that when phones are left unattended or are lost, this can enable others to have access to the images.

- If new partners find pictures from previous relationships they could become jealous and show them to other people.

- Remind them that if someone passes on intimate pictures of someone else to them, simply delete the picture. They should never forward the picture on to others. Not only are they showing empathy for the victim but they're also not attaching themselves to the situation. If they do pass on objectionable images, they become part of the digital trail that is generated and that can be investigated by the police.

- Encourage them to speak up if they believe a friend or person in their wider social sphere is caught up in a risky situation – perhaps being pressured or bullied, perhaps being sent a picture or maybe being pressured to send pictures – tell them they have the opportunity to stand up for others and the victim's family. They could talk to their friend, or they could tell you as the parent, tell their Lighthouse or a teacher at school. Encourage your child to speak up on behalf of others when needed.

- If you are worried about your child's safety, don't hesitate to seek help. Pages 152–55 have a list of organisations you can contact if you want more advice on how to prevent or deal with a situation involving your child and sexting.

STRATEGIES FOR PARENTS

What to do if your child is being harmed by sexting

....

- Remain calm, don't panic, and choose your words carefully. This will set the tone for how you and your family move through this event and out the other side.

- Keep the lines of communication open – this is the same child that made you poached eggs on toast for Mother's Day.

- Limit exposure of the event to younger members of the family. Choose a location in the home to plan and deal with the issue away from younger siblings, ensuring that the home still feels like a home for everybody.

- If you believe your child has sent a video or photo to one or more people, they should be encouraged to make a list of these people and then endeavour to contact the person/persons and get them to delete them. This is more effective when the content has been shared via mobile phones as the initial spread is limited, providing the receiver hasn't forwarded the content on to others.

- Turn your child into a note taker. If they get bullied by anyone, encourage them to make a note of the date, time and location and who said what to them. They should also record in what manner or context it was said (i.e., in class, by phone, a message online, etc.). This can help to empower them as they are now actively involved in protecting themselves and are powering up.

- When content has been shared via a social networking platform, contact the site and ask them to remove it. If you feel that you are not getting an adequate response keep resending your request until you get heard. State clearly that you believe the content is not in harmony with the site's terms and conditions. In most cases, these images or video will be against the terms and conditions of the site and they will be obliged to remove them. When you do this, let your child see what you are doing, or get them to assist you. You are showing them that action *can* be taken and it is not the end of the world. You are also modelling power.

- Keep back-ups of all communication sent and received from the online companies you contact.

- Encourage your child to lean on their friends. Often when a child has uploaded explicit images to the internet, friends of the child (real friends) react appropriately and offer support to the victim by comforting them and even trying to get others in the online social network to delete the images.

- Contact the principal or deputy principal at your child's school if you believe the content is being distributed to other students at school. They will want to stop this as soon as possible on behalf of your child, as well as other potential victims.

- Keep copies of all communication with your school, as well as notes about what has been said to you verbally, including the date and time.

- If you find evidence or believe that students within your child's school are circulating the images, spreading rumours or bullying your child, inform the school. Where possible, gather evidence such as screen shots of what has been said and show to the authorities at your school. Remember bullying is a crime and this can be investigated by the police.

- You can go to the police directly and get advice from them.

- As the parent you may have to do all of the above and at the same time look after yourself. Don't be afraid to ask for help. If you are losing sleep or unable to concentrate, consider seeing your doctor or asking a trusted friend to support you. The most important thing to do is talk to someone about how you are feeling.

- If you feel that your child is not coping well – perhaps they won't leave their bedroom, they've stopped talking to you or don't want to leave the house – consider offering your child the opportunity to talk to a therapist, perhaps arranged via your doctor.

- Your school may have a guidance counsellor or social worker who could also support your child while they are at school.

- Familiarise yourself and your child with how the law protects people under the Harmful Digital Communications Act. Having this knowledge helps you use the appropriate responses if confronted with a cyber-bullying issue.

- Only remove your child's digital device if you think they are likely to send more pictures or they are unable to cope with online bullying. Taking their device away is the last resort as this has the potential to isolate the child from their friends who could be offering support and advice.

- If you are not connected to your child via their social networks consider asking them if they would let you join them. Reassure them you're not doing this to judge or police them, but to support them.

- Ask them to let you have access to their mobile phones so that you can support them and keep an eye on what they are being exposed to. Your task is to find all possible ways to reduce the opportunity for cyber-separation to exist.

- Once you have moved through the event and life gets back to normal, stay connected to your child's online world. It is important to keep an eye on them to see how they are coping. Are they social, do they have friends, are they open and goal-orientated and back to the person you know and love?

- Contact Netsafe if you need advice and help. See page 153 for details.

Important information

If you believe your child is in immediate danger because of threats via any form of information communication technology, contact the police by dialling 111. If you are unsure, still dial 111 and they will assist you. If the matter is not urgent, contact your local police station.

CHAPTER 9

CYBER-BULLYING

Don't do it and don't let it happen to others

This chapter will provide you with strategies to help your child reduce the chances of being cyber-bullied, as well as ensuring that they do not harm others with aggressive or inappropriate behaviour online. As with all strategies to keep children safe online, understanding what their digital boundary is, using cyber-muscles and projecting family values will play a major role in contributing to their physical and psychological well-being.

Bullying is a complex issue and I do not believe we can eradicate it completely. I also believe we overuse the word so it loses its impact. **Bullying is a process, not an event.**

The definition provided to schools is:

Bullying is deliberate – there is an intention to cause physical and/ or psychological pain or discomfort to another person. Bullying involves a power imbalance – there is an actual or perceived unequal relationship between the target and the initiator that may be based on physical size, age, gender, social status or digital capability and access.

Bullying has an element of repetition – bullying behaviour is usually not one-off. It is repeated over time, with the threat of further incidents leading to fear and anxiety. Repeated acts of bullying may involve single acts with different targets, as well as multiple acts with the same target.

Bullying is harmful – there is short- or long-term physical or psychological harm to the target (e.g., as a result of coercion or intimidation).

Bullying Prevention and Response: A Guide for Schools[3]

It is common knowledge that in an issue relating to serious bullying, the child, teenager or adult expressing antisocial behaviour is themselves often a victim. When young people are living in homes that do not show love and compassion, with parents/caregivers who lack self-control, who are addicted to drugs or alcohol, who are suffering from poverty or a lack of self-esteem, then the child is often the target of antisocial behaviour, such as physical and verbal assault.

While it is true that when these children harm others they must be held to account for their actions, we should remember that as victims themselves, they require compassion and support to change their personal circumstances.

We also need to focus on our own child's ability to deal with issues of bullying and help them become caring, compassionate children, with the right to believe they can contribute to a better world.

An issue for society

Helping your child to understand the widespread nature of bullying will help them recognise it in its many forms. Being able to see it when it presents itself will increase their target-hardness. We need to teach our children that bullying is an issue society has to deal with and not simply confine it to what some children do in the school playground or when communicating online.

Children are affected by what they see and feel, and what they touch touches them, what they are exposed to affects them. Any environment that the child spends time in presents the opportunity

We are fed up with adults telling us why our age group bullies people. Adults bully adults, adults bully kids, somebody should do a doco on them ... just look at how politicians treat each other. Stop focusing on us and focus on the adults we are meant to look up to.

Seventeen-year-old teenager, Auckland

to model compassion, express tolerance, support collectivism and encourage self-control.

Schools are working more and more towards creating this type of environment, for example, when they promote cultural tolerance and teach human rights, they are modelling compassion and supporting collectivism. This will increase your child's inherent potential to support others in times of need. Ask your school what their commitment is to reducing bullying then find ways to complement this in your home.

Compassion in the home

Homes that model compassion and empathy will greatly improve a child's chances of living a successful life, and will do much to prevent them ever participating in bullying. Remember the boy earlier in the book who was too scared to tell his father that he had sent a naked picture of himself to a girl because his father, when watching a documentary on TV, had made derogatory comments about a boy in a similar situation, labelling the boy stupid and voicing the opinion that he deserved the chaos that ensued.

Imagine the positive impact if the father, in that moment in front of the TV, had turned to his son and reassured him that if ever he made the same mistake, he would still love him and be there for him to talk to.

We need to teach our children that the truest form of strength is the willingness to support others and to show compassion in other people's misfortunes. You cannot expect children to become empathetic because they pass a poster on a school wall every day that tells them 'You have the power to stop bullying'. To be successful at building empathy in our children and helping them learn compassion, it must continue throughout their lives. When we teach empathy, we are powering up our children.

I once watched a mother in a queue waiting to pay for her shopping. When she finally reached the checkout, the EFTPOS machine was down, and the mother started to shout at the young female operator, who had no control over the situation. The mother was rude and arrogant to her. Aside from the inappropriate way she was treating the checkout operator, there was a second victim of this behaviour: her son.

He was about 11, and he stood there watching his mother abuse another person. How might repeated exposure to his mother losing control contribute to his own lack of self-control when confronted with a situation that he finds frustrating, perhaps involving another student in a classroom? No poster on bullying has any chance of competing with his mother's poor parental modelling.

I recall many years ago walking along a busy street and in front of me was a young boy with his father. A few metres ahead of them was an old man pushing a shopping trolley full of junk, covered in a large plastic sheet and an old coat. He looked like he lived on the streets and was struggling to push the trolley because he was using one hand to hold up his trousers, which appeared to be three sizes too big.

The father stopped walking, quickly undid his belt, handed it to his son and whispered in his ear, at which point the boy walked up to the old man and gave him the belt. He accepted the gift, wrapped it around his waist and secured his trousers. All three chatted and the old man shook the boy's hand. The boy was beaming – as was I. As that boy grows up he is likely to be the type of child we want our children to play with and, eventually, the kind of neighbour we all want.

Children are born to care for and support each other in times of need – it's wired into their brains – and when we model compassion and encourage and nurture it in our children, we have the potential to make bullying redundant. This young boy is learning to live collectively and is being taught that caring for others is a strength. Never be afraid to provide opportunities for your children to learn to support others; it's the best anti-bullying education we have.

Mistakes can be made by anyone, sometimes with tragic consequences. Negative pathways can be taken by anyone, but children who grow up in homes that value love, empathy, compassion, tolerance and the collective good will automatically be better able to resist peer pressures and harmful impulsiveness, bullying or other negative behaviour. Through this ability to self-regulate they contribute positively to society, despite their youth.

Geoffrey Samuels,
Registered Clinical Psychologist

Parents need to be accountable for their child's behaviour

I have worked with schools, their students and parents in many cases of serious bullying, both subjected in person and online. During this process, I am aware of some parents who have had evidence presented to them that clearly shows their own children are the abusers but who refuse to accept the evidence, threatening legal action if the accusations won't stop and even involving lawyers. It is natural and right to defend our children when we believe they are innocent, but if the evidence is overwhelming, we need to tame the urge to blindly deny the issue. Instead, focus on what is best for the child. If a child learns that they face no consequences for their actions, they will almost certainly pay a heavy price at some point in their future.

In one incident, a father tried to defend his 14-year-old boy's criminal behaviour to me. The boy had repeatedly bullied another child to the point where the victim didn't want to attend school because he was too scared. The father's response was: 'In my day, that's what boys did; it was just boys being boys, and kids need to toughen up.' It was easy to see why his own son was expressing such antisocial behaviour. I pointed out that if he was unwilling to hold his child accountable for his behaviour, I would be forced to seek advice from the police. Parents have a responsibility to support their own children, but his dismissal of the seriousness of his child's criminal behaviour was not in the best long-term interests of his child.

Over-controlling parents

It is not uncommon among children and young people I've worked with who express antisocial behaviour online to find they live with controlling parents. According to these young people they are not allowed to make any choices for themselves about anything. They tell me that if they make mistakes, one or both parents rush straight to punitive responses, punishing them with consequences that are disproportionate to the mistake or poor choice they've made. The child will subsequently learn, when in the presence of Mum or Dad, to behave in the manner they expect and demand. A consequence of this is that the child learns to regulate their behaviour based on their proximity to the controlling influence, the parent.

If we train children not to do bad things only because they are scared of us, what happens when they are on their own? When the cat's away, the mice can play. Over-controlling reduces the opportunity for the child to learn to self-regulate, so they are more likely to express poor behaviour when the parents are not around. This is as true in the physical world as it is online.

Parents need to give their children the ability and freedom to make choices based on their age and level of maturity. They need to reward them when they do well and respond with principle and proportion when they make poor choices. This will help to make the child resilient, confident and capable of self-advocacy.

Cyber-separation: a nursery for cyber-bullying

Teachers on playground patrol at break times are there to provide support and monitor students. If a child gets hurt or seems distressed, they are there for them, and if conflict emerges they can help them de-escalate.

Parents who are part of their child's online world have the same opportunity as teachers in the playground. If they see their child saying things online that are inconsistent with the values of the family or appear to be harmful to another person, they can move in and support their child. It gives them the opportunity to remind their child that 'in our family we don't treat people like that, and maybe you should apologise'. It's a chance to support their child if they believe he or she has been verbally attacked. When you become aware early on of a bullying situation, because you or other members of the family share many of the same online spaces as the child, for example, this plays a major part in reducing harm. A family presence online is a major contributor to protecting our young.

It is also fundamental to a successful school partnership. I am aware of some schools that increase playground patrols on a Monday morning because during the weekend, students have engaged in online hostility towards each other. When left unchecked this can escalate into fights on the first day back at school. When parents abandon their children in the online world, the offline environments they gather in (like the playground) can become a nursery for cyber-bullying.

Young people get bullied in many different ways online. I have

> *I asked my daughter if she had ever bullied someone and she said yes. It shocked me. She said when she broke up with her boyfriend he found a new girl within days. My daughter said she couldn't stop herself, she would bully her online and at school. Then one day the victim didn't come to school. My daughter found out later the girl was too scared to come and was hardly sleeping. My daughter said she felt very guilty. She said she went to the school guidance counsellor to set up a meeting so she could apologise to the girl.*
>
> **Father, Taupo**

worked with children who have had rumours spread about them, and children who've had their identity stolen and used by the aggressor to send embarrassing messages and images designed to destroy their reputation. But in my experience, one of **the commonest forms of cyber-bullying, and one of the most harmful, is when** some children **deliberately exclude other children from online conversations and group experiences.**

In many of these situations, it is difficult for a child to react because the bullying is not directly confrontational, and it is not easy to detect as it exists below the radar of teachers and parents. With this low-level bullying, children often end up being socially isolated. They tell me they feel it is their fault, and that there is something wrong with them to cause this to happen. This can be very damaging to a young person's confidence and self esteem, and if it gets to this point, it usually indicates that the bullying has been going on for some time.

Powering Up

When a child is repeatedly bullied online, often they lose the ability to defend themselves. They lose their voice. One solution is to give them tools to respond to the situation, allowing them to connect with their own power. For example, Jordan, aged 11, is repeatedly bullied online and through text messages by three other students at his school. Jordan knows to follow the standard procedure of don't respond, take screen shots (gather evidence) and then place the evidence in a folder named with the person he trusts. An extra strategy with this, however, would be to encourage Jordan to print the evidence and place the screen shots into separate envelopes with the name of the student who is doing the bullying on the outside of each envelope.

Then, go with your child to the school and allow him/her to hand the information to the principal, deputy principal or whoever is helping to resolve the issue. This gives your child skills on how to look after himself. Obviously, the choice needs to be your child's as it is not a response suited to all children.

Turning your child into an **active bystander**

There is one powerful way of fighting this kind of bullying, and that is to teach and encourage your child to become an active bystander. This is a child who does not stand by and let other children suffer, who learns to say no, and will stick up for anyone who is being excluded or harassed. We need to teach our children that they have the power and the right to reject this type of bullying when it occurs.

When I work with an entire student body in a school due to an outbreak of serious bullying, what is often apparent is that if other children had stepped in, the incident would not have spiralled out of control. The workshop is called 'Strong Together', and it features a panel of students who engage with the audience in recognising ways to support and care for each other. They are often very effective because students experience their own power to speak and self-advocate.

In these workshops, we focus 90 per cent of the time on what the students do well. Students share what others have done for them, and how positive that makes them feel. In these moments, the students are experiencing what it feels like to live collectively.

The sessions sometimes include parents and other adults from the police and health sector, all of whom talk about the people who helped them when they were growing up. The police talk about the challenges of their job and what it means to protect and support others. Doctors

Three Year 7 girls made fun of my eczema on Facebook and they kept sending me text messages saying I was ugly. A Year 10 girl saw me siting on my own with my face in my hands. She asked me what was wrong. I showed her what they had sent me in a text message. She said she would look after me. She took me to the three girls and said 'You should be ashamed of yourselves. I'm going to the principal to report you.' I started crying. The Year 10 girl said, 'Don't worry. It's going to be ok.' I wasn't crying because I was worried, I was crying because she defended me.

Year 7 boy, Levin

talk about the impact of bullying on children and on adults they see in their practice. The students begin to realise that bullying is a wider issue than just schools and they see that even adults are affected by it. We will often invite parents to talk about the boy or the girl that stood up for their child who was being bullied and what that meant to them.

Out of school, there is a lot that families can do to encourage their child to be an active bystander. It is important to sit down with your child and identify the types of cyber-bullying and to be explicit that they are not to get involved in any antisocial behaviour. But you can also talk about the ways in which they can help and support other students who are being bullied. Let them know you will listen if they want to talk about friends who are being abused online, and that you will work with them to find a solution.

This is also a good opportunity to reiterate that online bullying is not in line with your family values, and to remind your child that **compassion and empathy are strengths**.

In order to be sensitive and aware of the signals that point to online bullying, and to ensure they know what to be alert for, make sure you

> *There are over 1800 students in this school and 99% are great people. How come we don't have research and posters that show that?*
> **Sixteen-year-old student, Christchurch**

and your child understand the types of cyber-bullying that can take place.

The most common forms of cyber-bullying:

- children being deliberately excluded from an online social group
- children having hostile messages or comments posted about them online
- children having rumours or personal information about them posted online or sent via email/text for the purpose of causing embarrassment or harm
- stealing a person's identity, and then posting messages as that person
- recording a situation in which the young person is being embarrassed or harmed, for example, videoing a person in a fight and then uploading the video for others to view
- threatening physical harm online

What to do if your child is being bullied online

- Children make mistakes and often a phone call to the parents of the person bullying your child may be all it takes. If you believe the situation isn't so serious, this may be a way to resolve the issue quickly and effectively.
- If the situation is more serious, ensure that under no circumstances should they respond or react, but repel.

- Teach them to take screen shots for evidence.

- Teach them to tell someone they trust, such as a teacher, a parent/caregiver, a friend or their Lighthouse.

- Don't panic or overreact, but listen and tell them they have done the right thing by coming to you.

- Secure the evidence, which can include text messages or screen shots from the internet. If the evidence is on a social network, don't delete this as the police may require access. However, even if those records have been lost, in most instances internet records can be traced.

- Inform your child's school of the situation. They will then be able to support your child, regardless of whether other school students are involved.

- If you know who the aggressor is, let the school know these details.

- Report the abuse to the website owners or telephone company. Keep resending your email if you do not get a response. Keep records of what they tell you and the person you've talked to.

- If you regard it as a serious form of cyber-bullying, report it to the police along with your evidence.

- If the bullying includes threats of violence, contact the police immediately. It is a crime to threaten another person.

- If you are unsure what to do, contact Netsafe. Keep records of what they tell you and the person to whom you talked. See page 153 for their details.

What to do if you discover your child is bullying another child

Remember that children do make mistakes. We can all think of things we have said, even as adults, that we regret, and young people are no different. In some cases, however, these mistakes can develop into long-lasting conflicts that encourage bullying behaviours. This is another good reason not to let cyber-separation form between you and your child, especially as they approach adolescence, so that any of these behaviours can be nipped in the bud.

It is also important to acknowledge those parents who are brave enough to listen when people present them with clear evidence of their child acting as the aggressor in a bullying incident. It is very easy to deny and dismiss these types of allegations, so those parents who have the courage to face them are genuinely invested in their child's long-term welfare.

There are a number of things you can do if you discover that your child is bullying another child.

- Find out why they are doing it, how long it has been going on, and by what means, i.e., phone, social media etc.

- Try to find out the type of bullying – is it relational, spreading rumours etc.

- **Ask your child to justify to you why they feel their behaviour is acceptable.**

- Explain to your child that bullying is not in harmony with your family values.

- Inform your child of some of the possible outcomes of bullying for their victims – this will depend on the child's age and level of maturity.

- Explain to your child that bullying can be a criminal offence, which could have serious consequences for them.

- Do not let your child make excuses for their behaviour. Stay in parent mode and, if needed, tell them how it affects you personally.

- When possible, and if appropriate, encourage your child to find a way to apologise to the person they have been bullying.

- Always tell your child how much you love them, and that this will never change, but make it clear that you do not accept their behaviour.

I received a phone call from my daughter's principal, who informed me that my 13-year-old was bullying a girl at her school using social media and text messaging. Later, during a meeting with the principal, he showed me the evidence. My daughter later dismissed the behaviours and just ran into her bedroom. To my horror, a week later the principal contacted me and told me it was still happening. I had tried talking with her about this, told her how much I loved her and nothing seemed to work.

I decided to try some shock tactics. I went to the local Police with my daughter and a police constable explained to her that her behaviour was illegal and could have long-term effects for her and the victim she was bullying. When we left, my daughter was silent all the way home and then, all of a sudden, burst out crying. I pulled over, put my arms around my daughter and asked what was wrong. She said everyone laughs at me at school, I can't understand maths and I hate everything. I hugged her and told her I would get her some help by talking to a counsellor at school and, if she wanted, a therapist arranged by our doctor.

Father of a 13-year-old girl, Auckland

STRATEGIES FOR PARENTS

How to protect your child from bullying

....

- Let your child know they can always seek help from you or someone they trust if bullying happens to them, and that the sooner they speak up about it the better.

- Teach your child *never* to bully anybody else. When a child has done this, the best way to deal with it is to firstly stop and apologise. Victims of bullying often say it's really helpful and healing to receive an apology.

- Teach your child to act quickly if they see bullying happening to somebody else. Some children are able to speak up in that moment and say 'Stop, this is not fair'. Others may need to tell an adult. It doesn't matter which, so long as they find a way to get help for the victim.

- Choose a scenario or even an example from the news and ask your child what they would do in that situation. For example, ask them if they were bullied online or at school by a fellow student, who would they go to report this? Then compare this to your child's school procedures for dealing with bullying (which should be on the school's website). If the child is 80 per cent correct you only need to add 20 per cent parenting.

- Teaching a child not to respond to harassment or bullying online is known as repelling, and is an essential strategy for protecting young people. Make sure your child knows that every time they do not respond, they become stronger than their aggressor, and that their lack of response is real power.

- Explain that it is important not to talk about personal things online or circulate personal information your child may know about others. Over-sharing information online can lead to a child or their friends being cyber-bullied.

- Teach them not to share personal information that has been communicated to them by a friend on to other friends and wider networks.

- Remind your child not to give out their mobile numbers to people who are not family or friends. Only people inside their digital boundary should have their phone number.

- If your child is being bullied via their mobile device, make a note of the date and time and if possible give the number the message was sent from to your telecommunications provider. They may be able to block the sender from your child's phone.

Important information

If you believe your child is in immediate danger because of threats via any form of information communication technology, contact the police by dialling 111. If you are unsure, still dial 111 and they will assist you. If the matter is not urgent, contact your local police station.

CHAPTER 10

PROTECTING YOUR CHILD'S ONLINE REPUTATION

Considering those who stand behind us

Your child's online identity, their digital footprint, is extremely important for their future career prospects, and generally for their reputation. Never has it been so easy for people to uncover information about a person's past, which is why it is crucial that you educate your child about the long-term consequences of what they post online. It is also essential they make use of security settings to limit access to personal content, in combination with making good choices about what they post online.

1982 versus 2017 scenario

Twenty-year old Chris Jones is looking through Situations Vacant in the *Evening Mail*. It is 1982. His eyes are drawn to '*Barman wanted for cruise ship. Send a letter of introduction and your CV to White Cloud Adventures* ...'

Chris has always wanted to travel so is keen to apply. With applications closing on 17 May, he estimates it will take five days to receive his application and CV, one day to process it and approximately five more days for them to reply indicating whether he is going to be interviewed or not. Fortunately, this gives Chris plenty of time to recover before his interview. He has a black eye and a limp, following a stag do the night before, where he'd got drunk, fallen over in the gutter, split his lip, bruised his eye and sprained his ankle. He recalls an ambulance taking him to the hospital.

Chris sends off the application and waits.

> *I was sitting in a waiting room about to go in for an interview. I got my phone out and did a quick Google search on my name. I nearly fell through the floor. My mate Danny had posted a pic of me mooning at a party.*
> **Eighteen-year-old girl, Dargaville**

On 17 May, head of HR at White Cloud Adventures trawls through the hundreds of applications for a bar person. One of their selection filters to cull the list of applicants is assessing the quality of the CV. She opens an application from a Chris Jones and notes the excellent CV formatting and his grades at school and she places the application in the tray for further evaluation.

Twenty-four-year old Chelsea Smith is in her final year at university, where she's doing a law degree. It is 2017. She is one of the top students and today her lecturer has told her that a large law firm, Pollock & Sons, is keen to meet with her. They were impressed with a project she presented to local law firms some months earlier.

The lecturer says they are keen to see her academic records to date, and does he have her permission to supply them? 'Yes, please send them,' she replies. The lecturer asks permission at 2 p.m., and sends them off directly.

At 2.45 p.m., Stephen, head of HR at Pollock & Sons, opens an email from his contact at the university. Earlier that day he had asked for a student's records because his director is interested in offering her employment, upon completion of her degree. He notes the name of the student in the email, Chelsea Smith, her academic records, the school she attended, and he has her CV. Stephen has to prepare a brief summary of Chelsea's 'real CV', which is a combination of the hard copy CV all applicants send in and a summary of her digital footprint.

He begins his search on the internet with Google images, placing Chelsea's full name and school into the search engine. He finds images of her playing netball for the school, in stage productions, and one of her in a newspaper article about helping her local community after an earthquake. This is looking promising. Chelsea is active, can hold an audience's attention ... the boss will like what he sees here. Stephen then clicks on one last image, which takes him to a page titled 'O WEEK 2013'. Stephen searches through the images, finding one of Chelsea. He is confident it is her, having found multiple images of her so far.

In the photo, Chelsea is sitting in the gutter, drunk, still holding a bottle of vodka. He notes the web address, right-clicks the image and saves it to his folder on 'Chelsea Smith', the same folder that includes her CV from her law lecturer. He decides to dig some more. He searches 'Chelsea Smith' on Facebook, Twitter and Instagram.

A pattern is emerging that shows Chelsea likes to drink and then loses control of herself. He finds posts she's made on Twitter, in online forums, some of which are opinionated and use language that is aggressive and often derogatory towards fellow students and lecturers. He records all of this into his folder. He already knows Chelsea's chance of getting an interview with his boss is dead. There's no way Pollock & Sons would risk damaging the reputation of their firm by hiring this law student.

It took ten days for Chris Jones to get his interview, based on what he had submitted, and it takes twenty minutes for Chelsea's to be declined because of content found online. Things happen fast on the internet. Chelsea had excelled at university and failed to capture an online presence which built on that.

With things taking time for the interview process in 1982, Chris wouldn't have to explain or answer to what happened and why his face looked a mess. Fortunately for Chris he wasn't born into a super-connected world in which every person he passes in the street has a camera; where his friends have phones with cameras they carry with them all the time.

When Chris got drunk and sat in the gutter with a bloody nose, his friend ran into the pub to get someone to call an ambulance. Without a phone, no one could record Chris getting into a fight, falling over, hitting his nose on the bar, being escorted out of the pub by the bouncers. Chris wasn't born into a world where every mistake a teenager makes out in the public arena or behind closed doors with friends can be captured.

The same cannot be said for your child. Whilst the internet doesn't judge us, it doesn't easily forget us. Your child's complete Curriculum Vitae these days is a combination of their academic achievements, work history if any, referees *and* their digital footprint. When your child applies for a job and sends their CV to a potential employer they will be subjected to an online background check. With so many applying, a company is looking for reasons to filter applicants out, before they start the interview process. If they find anything derogatory in image and/or text that relates to the applicant, the application gets removed. Then HR sends the applicant a letter informing them they were not successful, and your child would never know why.

Employers will look at images your child has posted, images your child's friends have posted of them, the type of friends your child associates with, blogs your child has contributed to, opinions your child has made, language your child uses and the tone with which they communicate. And in most cases your child doesn't get to defend or explain themselves if content found is deemed derogatory or inconsistent with the values of the prospective company or workplace.

Don't let cyber-separation form between us and our children. We need to stay in touch with technology, and teach our children to nurture and protect their identity; so they are always presenting the best version of themselves online.

Those who stand behind us – a personal story

I was being welcomed onto Murihiku Marae in Southland and my guide indicated that it was my turn to speak. He explained that as part of the pōwhiri, those greeting me wanted to know who I was, where I was from and who stood behind me.

I was struck by the respect they showed me in that moment. I was a complete stranger and yet they wanted to know about my family, and about my mother and father. This was only one of a handful of times that anyone had wanted to know about my parents in such a sincere way. I will never forget that experience, standing there on the marae, naming my mum and dad, acknowledging their legacy and presence in my life, over forty years after their deaths.

I had been asked to speak on this marae to their young people, to deliver a workshop on how to protect their online identity and reputation. It was a small gathering of around thirty teenagers, with some kaumātua and kuia sitting to the side.

Just as I was about to begin speaking in the wharenui, I noticed a line of paintings and old photographs along the back wall – their tūpuna, their ancestors. Their presence suddenly felt palpable; they seemed to be watching me. Something happened to me just then, causing me to change the content of my workshop. I delivered an entirely different message to what I'd planned. The revelation I experienced has sent ripples through all other aspects of my work, my life and how I teach today.

I started by reminding the students that there is only one of them on the planet, that each one of them is unique, powerful, and that they know where they come from. 'What kind of digital footprint do you think your ancestors on this wall, watching you right now, want you to have online?' I asked.

A girl at the back said, 'One that shows we respect them and that we respect ourselves'. From this point on in the workshop, we focused on respect for those who stand behind us, our family, our friends, and respect for ourselves.

I asked a second question: 'When you ask someone for permission before you take a photo of them, who are you respecting?' Another teenager replied, 'The person you are taking the picture of'. A boy then added, 'When you ask for permission, you respect the person, their family, you respect who you are and you respect your own family and those who stand behind you, your ancestors.'

One of the old kuia got up and walked silently across the wharenui towards me. She placed both hands on my shoulders, looked into my eyes and gave me a warm smile before kissing me on my cheek. Then she thanked me. I was silent. I felt emotional but very safe in that moment.

I noticed a change of atmosphere in the room. The teenagers sat and looked at me with a warmth I will never forget. They could see I was moved by what had just happened. We were all very aware of each other and a young boy asked me to talk about where I had come from. So I told them about losing my parents at the age of 13 and the hard times that followed. I told them about the people that stood up for me and I told them about who my mother and father were, and how much

I loved them. For the first time in my life in New Zealand I could feel my parents with me, and I knew who I was.

When a child knows who stands behind them, who they are, and that they are anchored to the values of their family, they will have respect for themselves and for others. If that respect is carried by them into their online world, then their digital footprint will reflect this.

The right to make mistakes

Always remember that your child has the right to make mistakes. This is a normal part of growing up, and when we discover that they may have allowed content to be uploaded to the internet which may hurt them in the future, we need to be careful not to catastrophise the situation. The lines of communication need to be kept open; judging them is not helpful.

> *My nana came to see me one day and she pulled out a picture of me drinking beer from a plastic tube at a party. My mum had given her a screen shot of me from off the net. My nana said it really upset her to see me doing this. She said, 'I love you so much.' She then handed me a picture of me sitting with my grandad when I was about 11, and he had his arms around me. She said 'If grandad was still alive, he would ask you to take the beer picture down and upload this one, so anybody who looked at you online could see how much you are loved.' My nana was crying. I put my arms around her and held her. I got my phone out and deleted the picture and asked her to send me the pic of grandad to put online. I knew in that moment why my mum and gran were upset.*
> **Sixteen-year-old boy, Hamilton**

Teenagers often remind me that the things they are doing now are just the same as what their parents did, the only difference being that their parents' misdemeanours weren't recorded for others to see. I'm sure we can all recall a social occasion when we did or said something that we regretted, wincing and cringing afterwards as friends or family members kept reminding us of what a fool we'd been.

Just imagine if that occasion was accessible online right now for anybody to see, and where they can form opinions about us. Just as we made mistakes, so will our children.

Use events in the news to target-harden them

From time to time news articles will report of people losing their jobs because of content found by an employer online. Other articles tell of employers who use online background checks during the vetting procedure. These articles are powerful to use because it is not *you* lecturing your children, but a third-person account and example of poor choices being taken. By informing them about real-life situations, you are empowering them to make better choices for themselves.

How to encourage a strong digital boundary to ensure your child's digital footprint is positive

- Encourage your child to stop and think before they post anything online as to whether it could hurt their employment prospects, and if what's being posted is in keeping with your family values.

- Encourage your child to upload content that shows off their commitment to others and their connections to the world. If they've helped others in the community, capture this and promote it. Remember, the most important brand online is your own.

- Be mindful about where you post information, especially personal information. It is one thing to post it into a social network that is 'locked down' with online friends you know who have access to it, as opposed to a publicly accessible online platform such as Twitter.

- Make sure your child doesn't create email addresses that are risky, racy or not in keeping with your family values. BassherBob@Yeha.com or LeggyBlonde@Yeha.com will not help them get a job.

- Don't create answerphone messages that are not in line with the family values. 'Please leave a message because I'm online bullying someone' will not help a young person get a job. Remember that what they broadcast will either work for them or against them.

- Teach your child to create profiles that are respectful and show self-control, and which *don't* use suggestive images or inappropriate body language. Encourage them to always stay inside their digital boundary.

- Your child needs to be consistent across all platforms that have their profiles on them. If they stop using a platform, they should delete it, and keep all instances of their online self up to date and relevant.

- Make sure the language they use or the pictures they post are fit for grandad's ears or eyes.

- Remind them never to attack others online who have perhaps insulted them.

- If they are in a bad mood, encourage them to get off their computer – never vent online.

- Demonstrate respect in your interactions and encourage them to do the same, while also being mindful of the things they click and like online. Are they consistent with your family's values?

- Make sure each member of the family is using privacy settings in their social media platforms to limit access to their personal information. Remember that these controls are useful but they don't replace common sense and family values.

- Ask them not to share personal things online even with close friends. Share sensitive information face to face or over the phone.

- Encourage your child to assess the pictures they're uploading or putting online. Keep alcohol out of the images; make sure any people in the background of the image are not hurting their reputation by association. Your child will be judged on the company they keep and how they act online.

- Before they send a CV to a potential employer, ask them to go online and search their name for what they can see about themselves. They should go through their online platforms and remove anything that is not consistent with your family's values or anything that may hurt their chances of getting the job.

- Suggest to your child that when they go out with their friends, they make a pact to not take pictures of each other if they get out of control or look vulnerable.

- Remind them not to send risky or personal content via text messaging.

- We all have a right to our political views, however, we should be careful how we express them, particularly to people with different opinions.

- Encourage your child not to comment on comments that their friends have posted if it's inappropriate. Doing this connects them to it and leaves them outside of their digital boundary.

- Remind your child that everybody is unique: our identity includes our family name, our brothers and sisters, where we live, what school we go to and much more. Our online identity helps tell the rest of the world who we are and what we're like. When we have a good online identity it helps us as we go forward into the future. It even helps our family members because we often have the same last name as the rest of our family.

I was at a netball game and a big argument started between two girls on the same team. A mother on the sideline started filming the argument. I couldn't believe what I was seeing. I told the mother to stop and think about how the girls and their families would feel if that was put online.
Seventeen-year-old female, Bay of Plenty

> *I got my first job over the summer break to save for uni. Full time and I was really scared on the first day but everyone in the office was kind to me. Three weeks into the job I had made lots of friends. I was at a party with my new friends and I got drunk. The next day at work everyone in the office knew about it from the images taken of me at the party because I had accepted my new work friends into my online social network. I felt so embarrassed I left the company. Look after yourself when you get your first job: it's an exciting time but you need to protect and respect yourself.*
> **Seventeen-year-old girl, Hamilton**

Maintaining a digital boundary in the workplace

This list is a reminder about keeping a positive, healthy digital footprint within a work environment. It is as useful to be reminded of this checklist for ourselves in our place of employment as it is to have this checklist for our children, when they begin to apply and be accepted for jobs.

- When you start a new job, consider when you will let new friends or work colleagues into your online social networks. Remember they will see a lot about your past, and much that is not in your CV. Keep your digital boundary in place until you are really sure about who to let in. Gossip travels fast in a workplace and you don't want to become the topic.

- Make sure you adhere to the employment contract you sign and pay particular attention to what you can or cannot say about your employer/company, online. Employees have lost their jobs because of failing to adhere to company rules when using digital communication technology at work and in their own time.

- When you walk through the door into your new job, don't bring in the same technology habits you have at home or with your friends. If you have a job that doesn't require you to use your mobile phone, make sure to not use it in work time unless your employer has said it's OK to do so. This is a major issue for many employers.

- When you go to a company party or drinks, refrain from taking pictures that are suggestive or could show your employer/company up in a bad light. If you took the photo and uploaded it to the internet, you may have damaged their reputation and your employment prospects with them.

- Don't let friends use your company's email address to send you inappropriate emails. Even receiving an improper video clip and forwarding it to colleagues 'for a laugh' at work can cost you your job. This can be regarded as an unacceptable use of a business-owned asset.

STRATEGIES FOR PARENTS

Helping your child with a poor digital footprint

....

- Remain calm, and choose your words carefully when you talk to your child. As you remind them about their digital boundary, ensure they understand that a poor digital footprint means they're placing themselves outside of that boundary.

- Get them to remove what inappropriate content they can, themselves. If the content is on a friend's platform, get your child to contact them and ask them to remove it.

- If you believe your child has lost control of the content and can't remove it, you still have options. You and your child need to upload positive content about them, pushing the inappropriate content down the 'pipe'. Time then becomes your friend, because as you and your child create content to upload to the net, along with content their friends post, the inappropriate content gets harder and harder to access. Positive content is surprisingly easy to generate. A child at a sports event, which is then posted onto their school website; young people in the newspaper being interviewed about something they have done; a young person on Twitter advocating something positive; teenagers going to parties and taking appropriate pictures of themselves and others enjoying life – these are all examples of positive content that can be used to compete with the negative content.

CHAPTER 11

CYBER-CRIME AND CYBER-SECURITY

When we over-share personal information

Parents are rightfully concerned about the spiralling rise of cyber-crime in our society, and the potential for their children to become victims. The highly sophisticated and complex ways that criminals use the internet is beyond the scope of this book, but there are still many things we can do to educate and protect our young people. If they grow up with an awareness of how to target-harden themselves and their families, it seriously limits their potential to become victims of cyber-crime.

All too often there are examples of how young people, through a lack of awareness, have enabled a crime to happen as a direct result of their online activity.

A child talks about going on holiday to his friends on Facebook. He also talks about the $5000 flat screen TV his parents purchased recently, and he uploads a picture of it onto Facebook. Before the family go on holiday, they need to find someone to feed their cat twice a day, so he posts a request for a cat feeder, online. One of his friends agrees to do this and asks for the street address, which the boy provides. With 600 'friends' on Facebook connected to him, some of whom he doesn't know, one is a burglar, who regularly prowls the internet looking for opportunities.

This boy was not target-hardened. If he had connected only to people he knew, set up security settings on Facebook that limited who could see his page, had not talked about family purchases online, had waited to talk about his holiday until he got back, and asked his friends face-to-face at school if someone could feed the cat, he would have avoided the heartbreak of having his home burgled. He would have stayed safely within his digital boundary.

I am seeing more and more children – as young as eight and nine – creating Facebook accounts. Many have hundreds of friends connected to their online profile, 90 per cent of whom they've never met, yet they share personal information about themselves, their family and their friends. This is a perfect environment for a predatory adult wanting to groom a child or a burglar wanting to target a home. We must pay more attention to who our children communicate with and to what extent they are sharing their and our lives online.

The key message for parents, both for themselves and for their children, is to minimise **the key contributor to cyber-crime: over-sharing of personal information**. This is either done willingly or through the use of social engineering, with people posting personal information into publicly accessible locations. As well, people often fall victim to criminals who manipulate and apply psychological

I was at home and the phone rang. I answered and a person said they were from Microsoft and could fix our computer. They helped me open my mum's computer and showed me the problem. They then got me to go to a website to download a program that would let the man from Microsoft get into mum's computer. I downloaded the application and then my mum came home. She said, 'Who are you talking to?' I said, 'The man from Microsoft is fixing your computer.' My mum snatched the phone off me and slammed it down. She went crazy at me and said I was talking to a criminal and how could I be so stupid. I ran into my bedroom crying. Mum scared me when she told me I was talking to a criminal. I'm really scared to answer the phone when I'm on my own now.

Eleven-year-old girl, Timaru

pressure to obtain information that may be used against them.

We need to teach our child about key loggers. Keystroke logging is an action designed to steal passwords and other personal data unique to an individual or groups of individuals, such as a family. The keystroke logger is a small software application, malware, that is covertly located onto a person's computer. This can happen after a person clicks on a link in an email. From that point on every key stroke generated by the person using the computer is recorded and sent to the criminal, from which they can then deduce such things as passwords and bank account details. To protect against malware, your child should refrain from clicking on links in emails or in text messages from unknown origins.

Cyber-criminals rely on people's lack of awareness and trusting nature. Often when a child is surfing the internet they end up at a website offering them something free, such as a screensaver, a software application or even the chance to win money or a holiday for the family. The website tells them to download the gift. When the young person clicks the download button, another screen appears which requires them to submit personal information including email address, full name and home address and more. This is referred to as a 'Squeeze' page. The young person has been targeted with a gift providing they supply certain information which is valuable to third-party applicants, marketers or even criminals. It is almost impossible to know the true intention of these sites. The gift cannot be accessed or downloaded *until* the information has been supplied. This process also allows identify thieves to place the key logger on your computer during the download of the free gift.

Teaching your children how *not* to share personal information is the key to target-hardening them from cyber-crime, both online and in the physical world. It is sobering how easy it is to obtain information that enables a crime to be committed. Information is everywhere. We need to leave out as much personal detail as possible when communicating online and particularly when in public spaces and forums.

We tend to believe that cyber-crimes occur because of something we do online, but that is not always the case. Sometimes what we do *offline* can contribute to a crime being enabled online. For example, when we leave letters, bank statements or medical details in a bin with personal details on them, criminals may use these to target people online.

This is based on a real scenario which happened in Auckland:

A café in a wealthy suburb of Auckland has a competition to win $1000. To enter, customers write their name and email address on the list provided, which is sitting next to the till. A new customer walks in for his coffee and notices the list. He quickly takes a picture of the list with his phone. He sits down with his coffee, Googles one of the names plus email address, and follows the search, which ends up at a blog site where people are discussing their expensive cars. The name this man in the café has followed is commenting about the Ferrari he has just purchased.

By using other personal identifiers in the blog site about this person, the customer easily discovers that he is the CEO of a large company in Japan. He searches up the company and locates its website. This type of information is invaluable to a criminal, and ways of using it are numerous. For example, the company website shows that every few weeks this CEO returns to Japan to attend to business commitments, which may encourage a criminal to break into his apartment when out of town, or steal his new Ferrari. All this is retrieved from a random email list on a café counter.

It's not only our kids who need to learn to protect their personal information. We need to be aware of what personal information of ours is being broadcast in an open forum in cyberspace. Cyber-crime isolates both the criminal and the victim. If the CEO is burgled, he would not attribute this to an email list on a café counter. However, he is obviously not concerned enough about where else he is disclosing details, such as blog sites. And organisations need to act responsibly, also. If that email list was kept under the counter, it would respect their customers' privacy as well.

Sharing the responsibility of a digital world

Avoiding viruses and **malware** (malicious software) requires **keeping your computer updated**. This includes both the system software, the operating system (the engine of the computer), as well as the software applications you use to be productive or do the things you enjoy.

Companies that develop operating systems and software applications are constantly updating their products and sending you updates to install. They do this to target-harden their products and, by association, you. Cyber-criminals rely on the fact that many end-users don't bother updating system or application software. Even worse, some end-users purchase pirated software that is unable to receive updates.

Once the known vulnerability has been shut down with the latest update, this doesn't stop cyber-criminals from trying to exploit that same system. In fact, when an update has been published and sent to the end-users, it also alerts the cyber-criminal to the fact that a weakness exists, so they are more motivated to target users who don't update their computers.

It is very important we teach our teenagers to update their computers as required. And remember, if they are using pirated software, this can put us at risk also – a digital life is a shared responsibility within a family.

What to do if you think your child has downloaded malware, especially a key logger

- Disconnect the computer from the internet.

- You need to 'ring fence' the infected computer, whether it is theirs or a shared family computer. Use another computer and change all passwords for the child's bank account, social media platforms, school log in details, etc. If a cyber-criminal has installed a key logger or has been given remote access to the computer, any changes you or your child make from the infected computer will be made available to the cyber-criminal.

- Remember that cyber-criminals specifically target children online, knowing many use the same computer their parent/caregiver uses to do online banking. When your child clicks on a link to get something free, they may well be downloading a key logger which enables a cyber-criminal to access bank account details or client databases. If they or you believe a key logger has been downloaded, inform your bank and have your computer checked by an IT expert.

- Complete a system security scan of your computer to see if you can locate the virus. If you are unsure how to do this, speak to your local

IT company. It's a simple process and they will be able to advise. It is worth considering having the computer reformatted, as this is the safest way to make sure the malware has been removed.

- You could also contact Netsafe for more information.

STRATEGIES FOR PARENTS

Helping children target-harden themselves and their devices

....

- Talk to your children about keeping you inside their digital boundary by not clicking on links from unknown origins.

- Teaching a child to protect their information begins by learning to value their identity. Ensure they're making informed choices about when and where to broadcast their personal information. This process is best started when they are young, and as soon as they start going online.

- Teach your child to be mindful of who they give their identity information to, including date of birth, their full name, mum and dad's name. Your child will need to legitimately provide this information from time to time, including home address and phone numbers to a health provider or a government agency, for example. This is fine. It is when they have simply clicked on a link while playing an online game to receive a prize from an unknown origin or while chatting with a stranger on the phone who wants them to complete an online survey – then they have offered too much information.

- Your child needs to know about identity theft. Identity theft is when a person takes somebody else's identity information, which could include full name, date of birth and IRD number, as well as other personal information including address, phone numbers and bank account details. The criminal then pretends to be that person, often with the purpose to steal from them. Cyber-criminals will search social networks looking for unsuspecting victims who may have uploaded too much information about themselves, their friends or family.

- Hard drives are known to fail, so teach your teenagers to make backups of their school work and personal content.

- Remind your child that cyber-criminals watch online communications and pick out the personal details that are of interest to them. To reduce the opportunity for this, your child needs to leave out all personal information when broadcasting online in publicly accessible locations.

- Encourage your teenagers to shred personal information before placing it in the rubbish bin. While this might seem over the top, criminals routinely sift through rubbish looking for personal information. Modelling this behaviour will encourage them to get into the habit of doing it, too.

- Teach your child never to submit information that tells the general public when they are on holiday to blog sites, chat rooms or social networks such as Facebook and Twitter. Knowing when people are away and for how long (as well as where they live) is a goldmine for burglars. This is particularly important for families with teens who spend a lot of time innocently chatting online.

- Ask your teenagers to check their bank statements regularly. Cyber-criminals steal account information and use a victim's own financial resources to purchase goods online and/or to pay for services without the victim's permission or knowledge. By checking their statements, they will be able to spot unsuspected or suspicious charges they did not make. If they see anything suspicious on their bank statements encourage them to talk to you and contact the bank immediately.

- Cyber-criminals often try to trick people through direct emails, by phone and text messaging. Tell your child not to respond to any message from an unknown person, especially if they are asking for personal or financial information.

- Teach your child about cold calling. Usually a criminal contacts the intended victim by phone and informs them that their computer is infected with a virus and that they can check or service their computer. The victim is instructed to give the criminal remote access to their computer so they can fix it. Once they gain access, personal data is stolen. Tell your child to simply put the phone down without even responding if they ever receive a phone call of this nature. If they actually talk to the person, they run the risk of becoming socially compliant.

- Criminals analyse photographs for personal information that a person was not aware of or did not intend to make public. For example, a child takes a picture of his dad's new jet ski, sitting in the driveway of their home. In the background of the photograph, the street name has been captured. If a criminal is in the child's network, he may look closer to learn when the family are not home and commit a burglary. Teach your child to either use a photo-editing software to remove this type of information, or, better still, think about what is in the shot and adjust the composition accordingly. Encourage them to do their best to remove any information that identifies the location of pictures.

- Smart phones, tablets and some cameras have the ability to store geographical location information in photographs being taken. The device itself adds the information to the image if location services are activated. When that photo is uploaded, you could be sharing the location of where you are, perhaps holidaying with friends, or perhaps a child sitting in their bedroom or a teenager at a party. This is fine as long as the images are not uploaded into publicly accessible online platforms. You can turn this functionality off by accessing the menu options or settings in these devices. A conversation with your local IT store or retailer would also be able to help you.

- Teach your child that before selling, giving or throwing away their mobile phone, all data needs to be removed from the phone, especially the SIM card. Many of these phones contain bank details, personal text messages, emails and images, all of which could be invaluable to scammers and identity criminals.

- Remind your child not to use free wi-fi accounts at the library or school to access bank accounts or make payments. These networks are unsecured, which can allow others on the network to access what they are doing.

- Teach your child to create strong passwords for their devices and their online accounts such as Facebook, Instagram and the many others they use. Reiterate that they should not share these passwords with anybody, even friends. Only you should have this information if it is required to support them online. Teach them to close their devices when they are not being used. This is particularly important in shared environments, such as the classroom.

- Ask them to password-protect any voicemail messaging system they use.

- Remind your child that banks will never ask them for their log-in details or passwords through email or text messaging, and that if anyone attempts to ask them for this information via this method they are most likely scammers. Repeat this message frequently.

- Discuss with your child that after major disasters scammers often send emails requesting donations, pretending to be a well-known charity organisation. Never act on this type of request. Always contact the charity directly before sending money. Do not follow links within an email or text message to do this. Try to speak directly with the charity and ask them if they are aware of the donation requests.

- Ask your child to always tell you if they have succumbed to a cold caller and given them access to any computer within the house. If they should tell you, keep your cyber-tooth tiger under control and work through the issue quickly and efficiently.

- You can also contact Netsafe if you wish to report an online scam.

Important information

If you believe your child is in immediate danger because of threats via any form of information communication technology, contact the police by dialling 111. If you are unsure, still dial 111 and they will assist you. If the matter is not urgent, contact your local police station.

CHAPTER 12

ONLINE GAMING AND PORNOGRAPHY ADDICTION

The risks of deliberate, repeated exposure

We are often able to recognise the signs that point to addictions such as alcohol or gambling. We may see someone staggering down the street during the day clutching a bottle in a brown paper bag, or we might know of a person anchored to a slot machine for hours and hours in a casino, and if we are connected to that person, we may be inclined to go to the doctor or another professional to seek help.

The context of the digital world is, however, much more complicated to read, as its maturation has been so fast and it has reached into every area of our lives, both professionally and privately. When a teenager sits in their bedroom doing homework on their computer, or Skypes their grandmother overseas, we rightfully see the use of digital devices as positive and acceptable.

The problem we have is this same location and device can facilitate a compulsion that becomes so powerful, it can have disastrous implications for the person. And the locations from which a compulsion can be fed are numerous: school, the bedroom, the car, friends' houses, walking to school, on the bus, using free wi-fi at a local library.

Examples of adults who have fallen victim to an online addiction are everywhere. There are parents who go online and play games day in, day out, trading away their parental responsibilities in favour of gaming, while it is not uncommon to hear of men who have become addicted to online pornography, and lost their jobs after being exposed accessing it at work.

The same risks exist for young people, and we need to do better at spotting the warning signs, particularly in those who may be at increased risk of becoming addicted to gaming or pornography.

If a child prefers to spend all of their time online, seems anxious, is often depressed, won't eat with the family, prefers to stay in their bedroom, won't go to school or starts to slip, academically, and won't stop gaming or alternatively watching pornography, then there is likely to be a problem and you must take some action. In these situations, it is important that the child or young person is referred to a therapist or child psychologist for support and help.

Online gaming – 'I'm a much better version of myself online'

Teenagers I have talked with often tell me they like themselves better online. A girl who described issues with her weight made an online avatar that she considered slimmer and more in line with how she wanted to look.

Many of the online games teenagers play are rich in context with realistic graphics. In these games, they have to achieve certain goals, sometimes with other team members. They get to choose what they look like, who they save. They get to right wrongs, they can become heroes, they are in control, and in cyberspace they have influence. Other players online like them and appreciate their contribution and skill levels.

But the problems start when outside of these environments they don't have the same influence in the world, things go wrong and life is far more unpredictable. For a young person who does not connect with other people easily, perhaps because they are extremely shy, or dealing with personal issues like weight gain or are being bullied, these online environments meet a need that the offline world can't. Teenagers who can't put the technology down tell me that online, they are the heroes: 'It isn't height and muscles that make you likeable online; it isn't the fact that you play for the school rugby team, which I don't; it isn't that you have the latest sports gear, which I don't. All of that means nothing online, where you are judged by how well you master the controls on the keyboard.'

A girl once said to me that she cannot run or play with others in the playground because she is so uncoordinated, but online she is one of the best players in her tribe and her team members love her. When teenagers in cyberspace get to re-invent themselves in an image they choose and control, when they find happiness online, it's not surprising that they want to be gaming at every opportunity.

Online pornography

Parents who have discovered their child is viewing pornography online and can't stop, describe a child who is stressed, anxious, who won't talk to them and has become secretive. I advise them to take their child to a GP in order to get help and support from a trained therapist or child psychologist.

It can happen quickly: the child mistakenly or otherwise clicks on a link and ends up viewing pornography, and then feels the urge to keep revisiting. It is important to talk with your kids, let them know it is natural to be curious, but that this can harm them if it continues. Keep lines of communication open – many young people tell me they have seen sex online but didn't want to tell their parents because they would get into trouble.

It is far better that they get it out of their heads into yours, so don't let your cyber-tooth tiger come out. Obviously most older teenagers would cringe at telling you about pornography they have seen online, but it is important that the younger children in your family are able to 'empty their heads' from time to time. Whilst they can't un-see it, talking with you or someone allows them to understand it is not a catastrophe. It also gives you the opportunity to talk about the risks of deliberate, repeated exposure. And it helps to reduce cyber-separation.

Adolescence is a critical time for brain development, including sexual development. In today's connected world, children and adolescents are commonly watching very, very explicit pornography on the internet. It normalises abnormal sexual activity, sets unrealistic expectations of what to do sexually, often glamorises brutality, and of course, consent is never sought. Sexual health providers see the damage on a daily basis. Of this I am absolutely clear: young brains need to be protected in development. This means that no young person should ever be exposed to internet pornography.

Annette Milligan,
Director, INP Medical Clinic, Clinical Director Women,
Child & Youth, Nelson Marlborough DHB

How to help your child avoid addictions online

- Talk with your child about the negative impact of too much time online, which results in the exclusion of other duties, responsibilities and pleasurable pursuits in their life. Start this conversation early in your child's life.

- Adopt a clear agreement about acceptable use of digital devices within the home.

- Talk about the negative health issues from living a sedentary life.

- Talk to your teenagers about the damaging impact that pornography can have on their outlook and health. It can skew a young person's idea of what a relationship is. Pornography tends to present an imbalance of power and this can affect how teenagers view real relationships. It is known to subsequently cause problems with sexual arousal in real-life relationships.

- Let them know that if they have concerns about their use of technology or what they are viewing you are always there to support them, not judge them. Let them know their Lighthouse is also a person they can go to. Introduce them to the organisations on pages 152–55 that are there to listen to them confidentially.

- Teach them that some teenagers prefer the online world because the offline one doesn't feel as welcoming. Talk to them about why this can cause some teenagers to become addicted to online games. Let them know that it's normal for any person to want to feel happy. However, addiction to this world needs addressing and resolving and the sooner the better.

STRATEGIES FOR PARENTS

What parents should do if addiction is suspected

- Note that the following advice is all subject to approval of a health professional, who should be seen as the lead in these situations. Always seek advice from a health professional, therapist or child psychologist.

- Limit exposure to the technology but do not completely remove the device. Remember your child still has to go to school and use ICT there and at home.

- Reduce daily use to a point that they can take care of their responsibilities such as school work. Check if what they are doing online is constructive and, if so, support it.

- Provide them with a mobile phone that sends and receives text messages only.

- Keep the technology out of the bedroom and in a busy part of the home.

- Pay much closer attention to what they are doing online.

- With your child's consent, talk to your school about the issue and find ways that they can support your child at school, sometimes by limiting access to technology when it is not required for school-based learning.

- Consider deploying monitoring and filtering software.

- Make sure you as parents are being taken care of. Talk with a close friend and think about seeing a therapist to get help for yourself. Many parents are deeply affected by a child with addiction issues and this is normal. You are not alone.

- Remember that, above all, your child needs support, love and access to non-judgemental parenting.

- And remember, you are not controlling them when you adopt the above strategies, you are supporting them.

CONCLUSION

Mā te huruhuru ka rere te manu
Adorn the bird with feathers so it may fly

If there were one unifying theme to emerge out of this book, it is arguably the importance of building resiliency in our children. And as the parents/caregivers in our children's lives, it is about us enabling them to have the courage to continue when things have gone wrong but, more importantly, to help them continue to do the things they know to be right.

It has been said that a whakataukī (proverb) will often be so accurate in capturing a thought or moment, there will be little need for any other words to explain it further. I feel that way about the beautiful proverb at the top of this page, which I use at the start of my workshops, and which I believe wholeheartedly is the essence behind keeping our children safe online.

It is up to us to give our children the feathers to fly.

We cannot realistically keep our children away from digital technology – that time has passed – and nor can we watch over every corner of their lives. We can, however, consciously choose to empower them with knowledge about the world in which they live. We can teach them about maintaining appropriate boundaries, about how to project power and confidence, and ultimately how to integrate good values and decency into all aspects of their lives, including when they connect with any form of digital communication technology.

I'm hopeful that you will encourage your child to use technology. It is an incredibly powerful tool that gives them access to this world that the previous generations could not even imagine.

It gives your child a voice, a chance to self-advocate, to speak up for others, to connect on a local and global scale at no cost and all at the same time. The internet never sleeps and it holds a potential that we haven't even dreamed of yet. It's no wonder children and young people like to be there.

The tools they use to traverse this space are just tools. The applications they download, the games they play and communicate in, the social networks they connect in all have one reason for existing: to allow the person to socialise, communicate and connect with others.

With this in mind, our task as parents/guardians is to wrap our children in family values and raise them with love, empathy and compassion – the feathers – so that they can go on to express these values in the hyper-connected world in which they now live. Your child's view of the world will be significantly influenced by how you treat them. Go well.

ACKNOWLEDGEMENTS

I wish I could individually thank each one of you with whom I work but I do acknowledge you here, collectively. I'd also like to mention some in particular who have made long-lasting contributions to my work, advising and educating me. Your support and encouragement over the years has made this book possible and you've played a significant role in how I work with children and their families.

I want to acknowledge the social workers from Oranga Tamariki – Ministry for Vulnerable Children. I know what you deal with and how much you care. I have talked with children and families across this country who tell me how you've changed their lives for the better.

Over the last 12 years I have worked in schools from Stewart Island to the Bay of Islands, from East Cape to Westport. The principals, teachers and receptionists I meet are amazing. I watch teachers, staff and volunteers prepare breakfast for children who may otherwise go without; teachers working long past their contracted time to support students and their families. And teachers who help and care deeply for children who come from homes that are far from ideal. You make a difference. Imagine if these kids didn't have you in their lives.

I work with Senior Net, Age Concern and organisations like Rotary that are committed to the welfare of people. I meet teenagers who speak up for others in times of need, and parents who go into the community and volunteer their time to support others. Thank you for what you do. Communities are wonderful things. Every family should have one.

Thank you to all the police officers I work with, who have influenced my work and education, and for your support and encouragement. I feel very fortunate to work with you. I get to see first-hand the positive difference a police officer makes when they represent children at their most vulnerable. I see first-hand the value of police officers delivering prevention-first, values-based education in schools. To Senior Constable John O'Donovan, who would have thought that from our first meeting over 12 years ago this would be the result? Quite simply, John, without your support, advice, and access to your vast experience in the police force, I would not be doing this work today. You showed me the importance of compassion and empathy when working with young and old. The weekly meetings with you to discuss cyber-safety education in schools and working alongside you in the community inspired me to not lose focus on the reason for all of this – to empower children to look after themselves. Working with you has been a privilege and an honour.

To Detective Neil Kitchen, Child Protection Team, Nelson CIB, thank you for arranging my very first police training workshop on cyber-crime. Working with you in the Safeguarding Children workshops has given me insight and professional development that serves me well in my work today. You have had a huge impact on the content in this book and undoubtedly on my career. Your statement 'Don't think what if you're wrong, think what if you're right', is what you ask of all adults who have concerns about a child's safety. I can tell you, there are numerous situations where adults, after hearing this, have been motivated to contact police or Oranga Tamariki.

I'd like to acknowledge Inspector Iain Mckenzie, Sergeant David Prentice, Senior Constable Phil Wylie, Inspector Mike Bowman, Senior Constable Jude Yeoman, Senior Constable Mike Tinnelly, Senior Constable Jos Sturkenboom, Senior Constable Terri Middleton, Sergeant Mathew Tailby, Senior Constable Pam Bell, Senior Constable Sam Cairns, Detective Sergeant Allan Humphries, Senior Constable Natasha (Tash) Marinkovich, and Senior Constable Deb Quested.

Waiting to present at a principals' conference on emerging adolescence, I heard Iki Valivaka, Greenmeadows Intermediate School, Auckland, share a proverb that made me reflect on my role as a father and as a person about to write a book. Mā te huruhuru ka rere te manu; Adorn the bird with feathers so it may fly. Thank you, Iki, you gave me the first lines in my book, and to this day those words still cause me to reflect.

To Paul Rodley, Director of ICT at Christ's College, working with you and your colleagues every year inspires me. The Colleges' commitment to the welfare of its students and staff has influenced my work. Thank you for your support and guidance.

To Douglas McLean, principal of Whakatane Intermediate School, working in your school and community every year is an absolute pleasure. Your passion for your students' well-being and safety is always at the forefront of our meetings. I cannot thank you enough for your assistance and support over the years. To Bev Moore (Statutory Services provider for Ministry of Education), you are a person I always rely on for advice and guidance. You've been a major contributor to my success, nationally, with your particular focus on the welfare and safety of children. It doesn't matter when I call, day or night, you are always available to support me. Thank you for all that you do in schools and for the wider community.

As with the New Zealand police, there are so many in education with whom I work alongside, and I'm very grateful to do so. Thanks in particular to Robin Sutton, Maree Shalders, Lucy Feltham, Simon Coleman, Rob Clarke, Alex MacCreadie, Henk Popping, Allan Mitchell, Alison Cook and Erin Cairns. Thanks to Helen Taylor-Young and all of the staff at Victory Primary School in Nelson for their support, giving me the space and time to test and evolve my teachings. A huge thank you to all the principals and teachers across New Zealand who have welcomed me into their schools. You have influenced how I work with students, helped me shape my teachings and made this book possible. Thanks to Kath Langman, Cathy Chalmers, Lali Hopkins, Kathryn Gray, Stuart Priddy, Trevor Jones, Justin Fields, Sarah Gibbs, Wayne Wright, Richard Barnett, Hamish Fenemor, Hamish Stuart, Marie Bramley, Carla Smith, Dallas Williams, Neil Wilkinson, Hugh Gully, Viv Butcher, Dean McDonnell, Kath Johnson, Ben Witheford, Kerry Hawkins, Richie Crean, Kevin Silcock, Regan Orr, Tina Johnson, Tim Lovelock, Antony Criglington, Ross Hastings and Steven Jackson.

My other main area of work is with the health sector, and I'd like to make special mention of a few key players in this field. To Willow Duffy, General Manager of Safeguarding Children, I have learnt so much from you and the rest of the team in Safeguarding, and continue to do so. Thank you for supporting me and providing me with continued professional development in Child Protection. To Annette Milligan, Director, INP Medical Clinic, Nelson, who has been a mentor to me for over eight years. You've played a major role in how I work. Thank you for challenging me and guiding me. Without your mentorship and tireless support, I would not be in this position today. Thank you so much, Annette. To Nick Baker, paediatrician, NMDHB, thank you for your contribution. I also want to acknowledge a couple of things you've said which I will never forget: 1) 'That if parents don't smile at their babies, their babies will not learn to smile'. This shows how vital it is we wrap our children in love and attention. 2) 'To consider when children are marinated in violence within the home as youngsters, what negative impacts this has on them when they're older'. This reinforces my aim to encourage stable, loving environments for our kids. Dr Giles Bates, your experience working with young people and your understanding of the negative impact that technology can have on young minds is something every parent should know. I am very grateful to you, Giles, for contributing to this book.

Other health practitioners I'd like to mention are Marieke Jansen and Briar Haven – I am always heartened by the compassion, respect and insight you show when working with some of our most vulnerable; Dr Andrew Munro, Dr Mikayla McKeague, Child Protection Medical Officer, and Dr Bev Hopkins. To Geoffrey Samuels, clinical psychologist, but also an overseer of my approach to cyber-safety education from the very beginning, thank you, Geoff, for your guidance and support and contributions in this book. I would not be in this position without you.

Within the community, I'd like to give special thanks to Kindra Douglas (QSM, Director, Victory Community Centre, Nelson). Kindra, you are one of those people in the world who make a difference to so many. You champion the rights of children and adults. I've gained so much insight from you into how communities operate, how people live and what they need in order to live meaningful, happy lives. Thanks also to Liz Price. As my friend and as a counsellor, you've often met with me and have a knack of noticing when I'm tense or having difficulties in my work, and you often seem to have the answers. Thank you for your wisdom and kindness. To Pastor Ian Wright, John Prendergast, Cheryl Smeaton – you bring no agenda other than wanting to get the job done; Karen Purdue, you are one of the hardest workers I know; Fraser Purdue, WRBT Charitable Trust: their three-year grant has allowed us to work long-term in cyber-safety education and your generosity has made a real difference to the lives of many families in Southland. To Paul Tuckey, thank you for your guidance, wisdom and friendship, and for welcoming me into your home. I look forward to converting all of your family to eating mushy peas. A sincere thanks to Southern Automobiles, Invercargill. Every few weeks I fly into Southland and work in the region and they supply a vehicle for me to use, free of charge. Number 10, Invercargill, you're doing such great work in your community; Saskia Walsh (née Nieuwlands), Heather Thomas, Janette Turner, Colleen and the team at Arrowtown Motel Apartments, Brian McGurk, Louise Faithful, Duncan Fuller, Patricia Fuller, and Tony Stallard. Thanks also to Geoff Mullen, you helped me understand the protocols and values that make visiting a marae so meaningful.

Thank you to the schools that participated in surveys for this book: Loburn Primary School, Christchurch; Burnside High School, Christchurch; Cashmere High School, Christchurch; Chisnallwood Intermediate, Christchurch, and Hillcrest High School, Auckland.

Harminder, you stayed true, a fast friend, a mentor and a guardian. Your wisdom and advice got me here. Thank you isn't enough for what you have done for me and my family.

To Ryan Clarke, Lead Developer at Xero Limited, such a close friend, you're more like a brother, really. We built the first simulated chatroom environment to help children make safe choices. You're one of the most honest, congruent people I know, and a gifted developer. Thanks for always being there when I need help, mate.

Paul Howorth, a close friend a Barrister a talented passionate man who cares about people and the planet. Thank you, Paul, for always supporting me and helping me see what's really in front of me.

The process of working with Robbie Burton and his team at Potton & Burton has been one of the most rewarding experiences I have had. The process of writing does not come easily to me; I prefer the spoken word over the written. Thanks to Jude Watson, editor, who has a writer's eye and a reader's ear. Jude, you made the book sing, thank you. To Robbie, since the day we met and discussed the possibility of this book, you've challenged me, encouraged me and spurred me on with your own passion for the book. Your ethics, view of the world and decency have had an impact on me, personally. Thank you, Robbie.

APPENDIX

NATIONWIDE SERVICES

Police and Emergency services call 111

Non-emergency contact your local police stations
You will find them in your local phone book or online

John Parsons: Workshops, Presentations and Family Consultations

John Parsons is available for parent, school, community and professional development workshops in your community, as well as keynote presentations in health, education and the private sector. He also provides confidential family consultations, in person or via webcam for families whose children are adopting risk behaviours or are victims of cyber crime wanting to re-engage with digital communication technology. *John Parsons does not provide emergency services so always contact the Police if you believe it is an emergency.*

www.s2e.co.nz www.johnparsons.nz

Child Matters

Educating to prevent child abuse.

Child Matters works throughout New Zealand, educating, supporting and inspiring adults to protect children.

www.childmatters.org.nz

Safeguarding Children

Working Towards Safeguarding Children. Tiakina nga tamariki

Offers an E-learning course in child protection training across New Zealand, helping people who work with children make a difference for kids they believe may be neglected or abused.

www.safeguardingchildren.org.nz

Ministry for Vulnerable Children, Oranga Tamariki

A new Ministry dedicated to supporting any child in New Zealand whose well-being is at significant risk of harm now, or in the future. They also work with young people who may have offended, or are likely to offend.

Tel: 0508 326 459
www.mvcot.govt.nz

Netsafe

Education, advice and support for parents and young people, relating to cyber-bullying, sexting and other ICT issues.

Tel: 0508 638 723
www.netsafe.org.nz

Ministry of Education

'Lifting aspiration and raising educational achievement for every New Zealander'

www.education.govt.nz

Lifeline

Provides 24-hour telephone counselling, as well as a leading provider of suicide prevention and intervention training.

Tel: 0800 543 354

Youth Line

Provides 24-hour telephone and text counselling, support and youth development services for young people.

Tel: 0800 376 633
www.youthline.co.nz

Tautoko

Provides support, information and resources to people at risk of suicide, and their family, whānau and friends.

Tel: 0508 828 865

Victim Support

An independent organisation that provides a free 24/7 community response to help victims of serious crime and trauma.

Tel: 0800 842 846
www.victimsupport.org.nz

Samaritans

New Zealand Samaritans provides confidential emotional support 24/7 to those experiencing loneliness, depression, despair, distress or suicidal feelings.

Tel: 0800 726 666

Norm Hewitt

Team culture and leadership development.

Norm is available for Keynote and speaking engagements

Email: normjhewitt@gmail.com

What's Up?

'I'm a kid and I'm keen to chat'; OR 'I'm a teen and I'm keen to chat' 0800 What's Up is a free counselling service just for kids if they need support or someone to talk to.

Tel: 0800 942 8787, Mon–Fri, 1 p.m.–10 p.m.; Sat & Sun, 3 p.m.–10 p.m.
www.whatsup.co.nz

The Lowdown

'Straight up answers for when life sucks'

Helping young New Zealanders recognise and understand depression or anxiety.

www.thelowdown.co.nz
Free text 5626

Mental Health Foundation New Zealand

'Staying Well positive mental health and wellbeing'; information on mental health conditions, where to get help and how to support those you love and care about.

www.mentalhealth.org.nz

Shine: Preventing Violence in the Home Helpline

Helping keep people safe from domestic abuse and family violence.

Tel: 0508 744 633

Women's Refuge New Zealand

Working to end domestic violence towards women and children.

Tel: 0800 733 843
www.womensrefuge.org.nz

Kidsline

NZ telephone counselling service for all kids up to 14 years of age, run by specially trained youth volunteers. Runs 24/7, but between 4pm and 9pm, your call will be answered by a Kidsline Buddy.

Tel: 0800 543 754
www.kidsline.org.nz

Plunket Line

Free 24/7 phone line to get help and advice about child health and parenting.

Tel: 0800 933 922
www.plunketline.org.nz

Health Click

The 'Me' series of resources: A series of social stories to teach people with special needs about personal hygiene, relationships and sexuality. Extensively used by schools, parents and therapists.

'Sex Smart': A resource used by schools to teach relationships and sexual health to adolescents.

www.healthclick.co.nz

NOTES

1. Sophie Domingues-Montanari, 'Clinical and psychological effects of excessive screen time on children', *Journal of Paediatrics and Child Health* 53 (2017) 333–338, © 2017 Paediatrics and Child Health Division (The Royal Australasian College of Physicians), Longdom Publishing and Qustodio Technologies, Barcelona, Spain.

2. Section 131B, Crimes Act 1961 [Section 131B: inserted on 20 May 2005, by section 7 of the Crimes Amendment Act 2005 (2005 No 41)].

3. 'Bullying Prevention and Response: A Guide for Schools', Ministry of Education, 2nd edition, 2015.